TORNADO: A COMMUNITY RESPONDS TO DISASTER

UNIVERSITY OF WASHINGTON PRESS   *Seattle & London*

James B. Taylor~Louis A. Zurcher~William H. Key

TOR

NADO

A COMMUNITY RESPONDS TO DISASTER

CONTENTS

ILLUSTRATIONS

INTRODUCTION

I T WAS THE CITY'S TALISMAN, comforting and protective. Rising above the southwest edge of Topeka, Kansas, the hill was known as Burnett's Mound. More than just a landmark, to the Indians it had been a source of safety, and their legend remained. It was claimed that no tornado could ever get by the massive mound, that it would deflect the force of any funnel. The belief was reassuring. Few people remembered, if they had ever known, that according to the dry and unsentimental records of the United States Weather Bureau seven tornadoes had in fact touched ground in Topeka since 1897. Perhaps the facts were easy to forget because these earlier tornadoes had caused minimal damage; tornadoes that do not destroy can hardly be real. Perhaps, too, it was easier to live with a comforting myth than a potential fear.

At 7:12 P.M. on Wednesday, June 8, 1966, the myth vanished forever. A full-scale tornado swirled unchallenged across Burnett's Mound. "There," according to witnesses, "it seemed to pause for a moment, and *increase* in force." It plunged down the hill and ripped diagonally across the city of Topeka. Seventeen individuals were killed, 550 injured, 1600 were rendered homeless. Property damage was estimated at well over one hundred million dollars.

After the first hectic days of tornado recovery, a new symbol arose, a symbol of strength and regeneration: an ancient cottonwood tree on the grounds of the state capitol. The cottonwood had grown from a twig used to anchor the guide ropes while the statehouse was under construction. In maturity it had provided shade for Presidents Harrison, McKinley, and Taft. The tornado left it battered, but its roots were sound; with help and surgery it would grow once again. Said the Topeka *Daily Capital*, "Today it is not quite so tall or wide, but it's going to take more than a tornado to write its final chapter." The change of image and symbol was clear: Topeka might indeed be vulnerable, but in spite of disaster the stubborn old city, with its roots firmly anchored in the soil of tradition, would rise and spread again.

Between the time when a comforting Indian myth vanished forever and the time when renewed confidence found its symbol in the living tree, eight days had elapsed. This book is about those eight days of disaster and change.

Why another book on disaster? Certainly there is no dearth of disaster description, of field studies, of social surveys, of scholarly reviews and conceptual schemes. "It is evident, then," says D. W. Chapman in introducing a survey of disasterology, "that the field of research on the human and social aspects of disaster has reached a state of considerable maturity of effort. The accumulation of data and knowledge is substantial" (Baker and

Chapman, 1962, p. 6). And so it is. Many disciplines and many viewpoints have contributed their insights. Baker and Chapman's book contains quite specific chapters on psychological functioning, mental health, family process, social systems, and community organization, all as they function in or are affected by disaster. Each behavioral discipline has made its specialized contribution to a specialized problem. In the field of disaster studies, as in any other discipline, such specificity and specialization is obviously necessary: the work of scholarship demands division of labor. But specialization also carries a danger. With specialization the ongoing flow of human behavior in disaster is compartmentalized, abstracted, and divided into categories by each scholarly discipline. But the events of disaster are not experienced as categories or compartments. Disaster causes psychological changes in human beings embedded in social systems; the social effects of disaster arise from the accumulated decisions of quite individual human beings; psychological processes, group processes, and political processes are intertwined so as to form part of a larger systemic unity. Social life, like life in general, "is a dynamic process —a constantly changing configuration of thoughts, feelings, and actions occurring in a social environment and continuing throughout life. If small parts and short segments of human affairs have to be isolated for detailed scrutiny, they must still be understood as parts of a patterned organic system and as segments of a lifelong process" (White, 1963, p. xii). A specialized focus on specific events in disaster tends to make invisible the patterns and interactions which characterize the organic whole.

The point is not that specialization or specificity should be abandoned in the study of disaster. Rather, we suggest that specialization and specificity are most valuable when they help us to understand the patterned flow of events. By fitting our bits and pieces of knowledge into the larger mosaic of the phenomenological happening, we are led to advance new questions. How do the social processes arising from disaster influence the reactions of individual victims? What individual responses lead to collective action? What are the effects of group action on the governmental process? How does bureaucracy affect individual behavior under extreme conditions? Such questions focus on systematic relationships in disaster; they cut across specialization and particular scholarly disciplines; and hopefully their answers can bring new knowledge and insight. It is with such systemic, interdisciplinary, multilevel questions that this book deals.

In these chapters we try to look in a unified way at a single disaster. We start by focusing on the individual actors in the disaster drama—the victims and the nonvictims. We try to show how the reactions of nonvictims and victims led to the emergence of novel group phenomena, and how group and mass behavior in turn was conditioned by pre-existing social structures. We then attempt to show how these individual and group reactions influenced the workings of social agencies and institutions, including the government of the city itself.

At each stage of the analysis we have tried to point up similarities and differences between our observations and those reported from other disasters.[1] Further, we have attempted to show how the social processes—the social dynamics—observed in the disaster situation are similar to those found in other situations which call forth collective behavior. Thus in this single volume we move from a microscopic focus on the individual response to a macroscopic focus on historical behavior under conditions of stress.

In order to understand the impact of disaster as an organic unity, we have emphasized the adaptive, purposive nature of behavior on both the individual and the collective levels. Our concern is with the task-focused, goal-oriented causes of human action, whether that action takes place in persons, in groups, or in organizations. Thus the research reported in this book is personal-

---

[1] The reader should be forewarned that the comparisons are largely illustrative, designed to show that the described events were not idiosyncratic to Topeka. We have not here attempted the exhaustive task of reviewing all the relevant and voluminous literature of disaster.

istic and highly case centered. It deals with the raw data of personal experience. We have allowed the participants to speak for themselves, to tell it as it was for them. The words of our informants communicate, better than any writer could, the sight, smell, and chaos of the stricken city; the grim struggles of survival and renewal; and the very human processes by which people overcome—or sometimes fail to overcome—adversity.

At the time the disaster struck, the authors of this volume were engaged in various social-psychological research efforts in Topeka. In the course of their work they had become intimately familiar with the city and its citizens. Dr. William Key, a fourteen-year resident of Topeka, was surveying the impact of urban renewal; his long-time participation in community affairs allowed him to deal in friendly and familiar terms with many political and agency leaders. Dr. Louis Zurcher was studying the birth throes of the local Office of Economic Opportunity (OEO) program; his work provided another kind of entree. Dr. James Taylor was directing a personality-oriented study of work and its vicissitudes among low-income families. These projects provided a background of information and experience which threw certain aspects of the disaster into bold relief.

When the tornado hit, all three became involved in the recovery efforts. Research was laid aside for a while as the vivid needs of a wounded city took precedence. But in the course of these recovery efforts, all three became convinced that they were viewing a unique and unexpected social process which merited investigation. In the wake of the disaster, a host of new social structures and social roles were emerging. The dynamics of this social process seemed fascinating, important, and at times obscure. Here was something which needed to be studied in depth.

On June 15, 1966, when volunteer help was no longer needed, the authors began a series of unstructured interviews with city officials, news media representatives, professional disaster officials, volunteers, victims, ministers, behavioral scientists, and with any other individuals who had played a part in the recovery efforts. These interviews generally lasted from one to three hours, and in most cases they were tape recorded. Some volunteers and victims contributed their own diary reports, often made within a day after the tornado. Altogether, 101 such reports or interviews were gathered. In order to increase understanding of individual reactions, ten psychotherapists at The Menninger Foundation were asked to review all of their therapy cases, the review focusing upon patients' behavior and motivation immediately after the disaster. In sum, the following data were collected:

30 interviews or diary reports from adult victims
6 interviews with adolescent victims
7 reports on preschool age victims, as seen in a nursery school
24 interviews or diary reports for volunteers
16 interviews with agency heads or government leaders
10 case review sessions for Menninger Foundation psychotherapists, giving in-depth data on 10 victims, 11 helpers, and 16 nonhelpers
2 interviews with newsmen and television reporters
16 interviews with previously studied families in the low-income area of Topeka

In addition, television station WIBW provided access to videotape records of their broadcasts during the tornado period, and many agencies provided copies of their retrospective reports on the disaster. Except for the psychotherapists' interviews, the great bulk of this information was gathered within three weeks of the tornado. The therapists were seen four to six weeks after the disaster; usually patient reactions could be reconstructed from notes taken during the post-tornado therapy hours.

The authors also had first-hand experience with volunteer recovery efforts. Zurcher, as a "foreman" of a volunteer work crew, recorded field notes during and immediately after the work day—in no case longer than twelve hours after the observations were made. He also conducted interviews with the work crew volunteers, eight being completed within one week of the tornado, and one after three weeks. These participant observations and interviews form the basis for Chapter 4, and in a somewhat different form have appeared in prior publication (Zurcher, 1968).[2] Key helped manage a volunteer center; his experiences led him to study the governance of the city during the disaster period, a study whose results are reported in Chapter 6. The other portions of the book are predominantly the product of the senior author.

This volume would not have been possible without the assistance of many colleagues who helped to gather material and who contributed ideas and criticism of our efforts. First and foremost, we acknowledge the stimulation of Dr. Gardner Murphy, without whose kindly encouragement and no less kindly prodding this book would not have been written. We are grateful to The Menninger Foundation for providing the funds which made the research possible. For interviewing and observational materials we are indebted to Doctors Lois and Gardner Murphy, Alice Moriarty, Robert Harder, Robert Simpson, Herbert Modlin, Harold Voth, Richard Siegal, Clark Case, Jerome Katz, Irwin Rosen, David Rosenstein, William Tarnower, Robert Menninger, Fernando de Elejalde, and Ronald Filippi; and to Mrs. Virginia Feeley, Beth Sheffel, Jennie Wykert, Mr. Courtney Jones and Mr. Alvin Green. Among the research assistants who conducted interviews our thanks go to Mr. Fred Hill, Miss Marianne Ptacek, Miss Rosanne Barnhill, and Mr. Joseph Morgan. Mrs. Martha Carithers served as an able and surprisingly patient editorial assistant. We are grateful for the conscientious efforts of our secretaries, Mrs. Geneva Vonderschmidt, Mrs. Mary Prosser, Miss Janice Boldridge, and Mrs. Sherry Schiller, whose work was a model of efficiency under pressure. Television station WIBW kindly made available to us their transcriptions of the tornado news broadcasts, and the Disaster Research Center, of Ohio State University at Columbus, gave us access to their rich bibliographic

---

[2] A portion of Chapter 1 has also appeared in that same publication.

resources. We are especially indebted to Dr. E. L. Quarantelli of that center for his thoughtful comments and suggestions.

But our major gratitude goes to the citizens of Topeka, without whose willing and gracious help this volume would not have been possible.

TORNADO: A COMMUNITY RESPONDS TO DISASTER

Topeka, the capital city of Kansas, is located seventy miles west of Kansas City. Covering a land area of 12.5 square miles, the town is known for its wide streets and avenues, and its well-shaded residential areas. Various governmental agencies provide the leading source of employment, along with agricultural processing and manufacturing. The Menninger Foundation, working cooperatively with state and Veteran's Administration facilities, has made the city a national center for treatment, research, and education in mental health. Population in 1960: 119,484, of which 92 percent were categorized as "white" by the census.

CHAPTER ONE

TOPEKA, JUNE 8, 1966

O BILL KURTIS, the television announcer at Topeka's WIBW studio, the evening of June 8 began with springtime calm. A law school graduate, Kurtis had spent the preceding three weeks studying for his bar examination; this evening he had put his books aside to substitute for another newscaster. He arrived at the station just after a tornado watch had been broadcast. The warning was out: this was tornado weather. In Kansas tornado watches are common: WIBW had broadcast fifty or more within the year. Usually nothing came of them. Bill Kurtis, like most Topekans, was skeptical; no tornado had ever damaged the city.

The first tornado report came from the town of Manhattan, Kansas. As Kurtis described it later:

> It was a report of high winds, very damaging winds. This was about 6:20 or 6:30. So we started assembling damage reports from Manhattan. A sailboat had been thrown clear down the street, and windows were damaged. They didn't know the extent of it then. So we were all keyed up and really in operation because of the Manhattan storm. We were on the air about ten till seven, giving disaster reports from Manhattan.

The town of Manhattan lies fifty miles west of Topeka. The usual tornado path is from southwest to northeast; that storm might therefore be expected to move toward Topeka, but it did not. Instead came word of a different funnel:

> About five till seven we received a report from Ed Rutherford, one of our photographers, that there was a tornado on the ground southwest of the city of Topeka. Then the Weather Bureau confirmed it, and said that they had a definite radar picture, and it was heading towards Topeka. At that moment, we made the decision to go on the air and stay on. This was the closest, really, that we had been to a tornado for a couple of years. We always had alerts but none really this definite.

What Ed Rutherford had seen on the ground, and the weatherman on his radar screen, was both common and dreaded. Although its destruction is less extensive than a hurricane, a tornado is uniquely devastating within its limited range—a sniper's bullet compared to a shotgun blast. It is like no other storm on earth. The *Encyclopedia Britannica* (1957, p. 301) describes it thus:

Tornado. The violent revolving funnel-cloud of small diameter that is well-known in the United States east of the Rockies. . . . In North America, tornadoes average 300–400 yards in width, although some extend a mile or more. They often form in families of two or more in the same region at the same time. Paths are short, from several to 50 miles, rarely as much as 300 miles long; in the United States they generally run from southwest to northeast at 10–50 miles per hour. . . . . The whirling funnel cloud appears to grow vertically or slanting down from the base of a dark heavy cloud of the cumulonimbus or thunderstorm type and reach the ground twisting and bending slowly, the base dragging because of friction. . . . Rain and hail usually occur just before or after the tornado.

Certain regularities, not completely understood, are typical of tornadoes. Usually they occur in late afternoon or early evening. Before they develop the sky often has a sickly yellow-green cast. In the central United States they arise especially when a cold dry mass from the north Pacific coast comes into collision with hot and humid air from the Gulf of Mexico. The sudden condensation within the saturated atmosphere, the boiling of the winds as cold clashes with heat, the bubbling and swirling of the air, releases enormous energies which sometimes find form in circular whirling winds of unique violence. The sheer power of the tornado has never been accurately defined or measured. The winds within the central funnel move at speeds estimated up to five hundred miles per hour. In the whirling mass a partial vacuum is formed, so that across the path of the tornado houses explode outward, roofs crack and fly away, and high in the air the clouds glitter with debris. It was this phenomenon which touched the ground on June 8 and moved toward the city of Topeka, Kansas.

The tornado first appeared near the small town of Auburn, twelve miles southwest of Topeka. Beginning as a flimsy white column fifty yards in diameter, it damaged a few farm buildings, a house trailer, and some fences. An elderly farm couple, Mr. and Mrs. Calvin Wolfe, failed to see its approach; their neighbors were more fortunate:

> We heard this warning, saying there was a twister on the ground on the road. We immediately looked out our southwest window. As near as I could tell this twister was 300 feet from us. We took our bird—and the cage—and made it to the basement. Just barely got down on the floor in the southwest corner when it hit. It just really broke loose when it did hit. And as soon as it was over we came out of the

basement and found the house next door, where the Wolfe's
had lived, almost completely gone. It just picked up the
house and carried it across the road and dropped it. They
didn't have warning enough. If they had even thirty seconds
they could have made it to our basement. They always said
they would so I'm sure they didn't get any warning. [It was
too late; the Wolfes were dead.]

In the WIBW newsroom other reports on the tornado were
coming in. Kurtis remembered later:

> There was a sighting from Burnett's Mound. Then we
> got two other reports, one from 21st and Wanamaker, and
> another one from the south about two miles. This means then
> that three tornadoes were converging on Topeka. And going
> through my mind I was thinking, "Well, it may have been
> the same tornado reported from these different locations."
> Often that's the case when things get hot and hairy, you put
> it on the air, and you don't wait for it to be verified because
> you have to get it on right then.

But quickly the reports became clear: a large funnel was sighted
southwest of Topeka, and it was approaching Burnett's Mound:

> This was a pretty tough spot because it was on the
> ground and headed into the southwest portion of the city.
> So, what to do? You know it's going to hit and you know it
> probably has hit. I decided to give a warning to the rest of
> the city, all the time not dreaming that this thing would be
> on the ground and remain on the ground through the whole
> city.

Topeka had an established routine to warn of tornadoes. A
tornado watch meant to the citizens that tornadic conditions
existed; a tornado alert meant that a funnel was in the area.
When a tornado alert is declared the city's air raid sirens sound.

The tornado alert sirens blew as most people were at home
finishing dinner. They caused no panic; the predominant feeling
was "there they go again." Many Topekans had developed the

habit of staying above ground when they heard the sirens. Somehow that day was different. By and large, most took shelter. The difference was many-faceted. In part it lay in the weather itself; the sky had a greenish and foreboding tinge. There were the cautionary reports from Manhattan, where a real storm had struck and damage had been done. And the hour made it easy to get up from the dinner table and go to the basement; during the five o'clock rush hour things might have been different. Beyond this, many people noted an air of urgency in the reports on radio and television. The announcer's voice was breathless; the reception was punctuated with sharp static from electrical interference. Most people either turned on their radio or were warned by those who had.

THE STORM

The tornado could be seen coming over Burnett's Mound. One man reported:

> It did not have the classical tornado shape. Over in the Burnett Mound area the sky came down to the ground like a very wide column. We watched this and all of a sudden we started seeing what looked like millions of birds inside this column. It was the debris in the air. Then we began hearing the roar. It was coming at a pretty good clip, two or three blocks wide, and all of this debris coming out of the side of it. It had a gray, heavy-rain look: it was not black and certainly did not have the snake-like shape that you usually imagine. The fellow across the street is a retired Air Force man, and I said to him, "Boy this looks like a good one!" You could tell by the way the debris was coming and the noise of it that it was one hell of a funnel.

The storm was often heard before it was seen. Many described the sound as like a roar of a freight train; others reported that they heard (mingled with the roar) a high-pitched whine as of a jet plane overhead. Those close to the storm's path were also conscious of the sound of falling debris: one man came up from the basement thinking he was in a hailstorm, and found instead a shower of bricks, stones, and wood raining from the sky above.

Initial reaction was often one of disbelief. People did not *really* expect the tornado to strike; when it did strike they had difficulty in believing that it was real; and afterward it was hard to believe that it had taken place. A young reporter from the local newspaper tells what happened to him at 7:15 P.M.:

> All I knew was what I could see out of the small window in the *Capital* newsroom. I saw it pick up a tree and break it in two, and I saw stuff flying past the window, and I felt the building shake, and I heard the roar. But I really didn't think it was a tornado; I don't think anybody really thought that it was a real tornado hitting us there in the *Capital-Journal* building.

Often it was not until the next day, when the devastation was seen first-hand, that it was believed.

This reaction—disbelief even in the face of experience—is common. Research on the Marysville and Yuba City floods of 1955 found that "39% of those who remembered receiving warning reports indicated that they did not fully believe them" (Blum and Klass, 1956, p. 43). Similar disbelief was reported by Moore (1958) among tornado victims, and by William Menninger (1952) for the Topeka flood. As Withey (1962, p. 113) points out for all disasters, "there is a tendency for new stimuli to be interpreted within a framework of the known and familiar. . . . Under conditions devoid of threat and stress, if threat cues are introduced, the tendency will be to interpret them as unthreatening until such interpretation can no longer be made." This was clearly the case in Topeka: few people expected a tornado to come, but the danger if it *did* come was great. So people took shelter in spite of disbelief.

Perhaps to counter this feeling of disbelief, as well as to experience such an unusual phenomena, many people attempted to view the tornado—occasionally even at the risk of their own life. A sixty-six year old Negro lady in the East Topeka area reported this reaction:

> A man jumped out of a taxi and ran into the house and said, "There's a tornado!" And I said, "Well, let me go out and look," and I looked up and I saw it too. Then I called to him to come and look and he wouldn't do it. He run and grabbed me by the arm and slammed the door.

An elderly Mexican man, who as a youth had fought in the army at Pancho Villa, refused to seek shelter. He explained later he wanted to see for himself the face of God. Shelter, he said, was for women and children.

Often disbelief was maintained to the very last moment. Said one girl, "I still didn't believe anything was happening until I looked back over my shoulder—and there the tornado was." Another lady was quite vehement in rejecting the total idea: "Stupid things like tornado reports, you just really can't take them seriously."

THE SHELTER

In the shelters it was common for the victims to huddle together for reassurance. Often the men would attempt to protect their families by lying across them. Panic was rare. Typically, the victims sat mutely, or tried to calm the few people who became visibly upset:

> I didn't have any fear; I didn't really think I was going to be blown away. I know I was disturbed but there was really no hysteria. My thirteen year old daughter was quite scared. When it began to blow pretty hard she crawled under some screens that were leaning in the corner of the basement. She stuck her hand out to me and started crying hysterically. And I said, "Now just calm down. If the Lord wants us now, we are probably just as ready as we'll ever be." And I said, "If you ask Him, He'll save us." And she quieted down then.

By calming others, the victim also calmed himself:

> I could sense the second the worst was over and I said, "Don't worry the worst is over. It's going, it's going. It's going to be over in a second." I said that very loudly to everyone. It was to reassure myself.

At the height of the storm people generally huddled in silence:

> The roar kept getting worse and worse, and I think that during the worst part of the roar none of us said anything. It seemed it was a long time before the roar diminished. I knew it had to pass over, and I kept waiting for it to become silent; but it seemed like it stayed and stayed. And after it diminished some, you could hear the crashing and the glass and oh so many sounds. At the height of the roar it felt like there was a suction in your ears, as if there was a pulling in your eardrums.

The muteness, the lack of panic remained after the tornado had passed. Again, no panic, even when it looked as if the victim was trapped and lost. One girl described such an episode:

> All this debris had fallen down the stairwell into the basement and we couldn't get out. The men there of course tried to push out from underneath and they couldn't. People started to get more panicky then. We looked up at the ceiling and saw that it was caving in: plaster had fallen in, and it looked as if there were sheets up there with water in them. We could smell gas, maybe from the gas main from the apartment. And the water was pouring out of the burst pipes, and I thought, "O my God, if we can't get out we'll get drowned." But no one got really hysterical, and the men tried to push the stuff aside. They had no success but there was some light coming in. Eventually people came from above and started lifting stuff off. It took quite a while. After they got everything off, the stairwell was gone and we still had to get up to the ground.

The funny thing was that the people who were above helping us . . . no one said a word, they just started pulling people out. They would only say, "Easy now. Watch your step." There were no other comments made by any of them as the people got out, one by one. No one remarked on the destruction.

EMERGENCE

After the storm came an eerie kind of surrealistic calm. The victims emerged into a changed landscape. To some, freshly escaped from death, the most noticeable thing was the beauty of the world:

> After the storm was over we went outside. It was very hot and still—no wind. The sky was very blue and the sun was setting and it was really quite lovely.

To others, the changed and shattered landscape was tragic. Water gurgled from broken pipes; the air smelled of gas and plaster dust; trees thrust jagged stumps against the flattened horizon; mounds of rubble lay where proud houses had stood. It was too much to comprehend:

> After we came out I had a feeling of disbelief, like a bad dream. I was saying to myself, like, "Oh, this just can't be." It happens too quick for you to comprehend at the moment. It just seems as if you were maybe looking at a picture. It doesn't touch you personally. You feel the same way you feel when you look at pictures of other areas that have had destruction. It isn't real to you.

With the sense of unreality came attempts at denial:

> All of my neighbors' houses were gone—all of them. Oh, some of them had portions of walls, but almost all of the rubble was piled right on top of the basement. And—to show how illogical your thinking is at such times—I said, "Well, I know they'll be all right. They've all got basements." Even though I knew they had two stories of rubble on top of them.

At the WIBW newsroom accounts of destruction jammed the switchboard. The news staff gave separate reports to Bill Kurtis, who stood before the television camera and tried to make sense of the disaster. It was not an easy task:

> We had a report at Washburn University. The campus had been hit. That's all we had. Then we had a report from 10th and Topeka. Then a report that it went across the Interstate Highway south of Ramada Inn. Then through the Santa Fe Shops. . . . All the time not dreaming that this thing would be on the ground and remain on the ground through the whole city. I could just see it lifting back up in the air. . . . Nobody realized that this thing was on the ground until the next morning when they started counting the places it had hit.

It was natural to believe—and hope—that the tornado had touched the city only here and there. The facts were otherwise.

The tornado had entered in the southwest corner and disappeared to the northeast, leaving behind it a four-block wide and eight-mile long swath of destruction ripped diagonally across the city. Nothing had been spared. A luxury apartment complex lay in ruins; the local university was reduced to rubble; miles of homes were damaged or destroyed; venerable houses which had sheltered generations of Topekans, stood with walls half gone and window screens bulging out like sails in a high wind. In the car barn of the local transit system the busses lay piled together like crushed and discarded beer cans. A ten-story office building in downtown Topeka was left windowless, its interior gutted. East of the Santa Fe tracks, in a working-class neighborhood, families found themselves roofless and homeless. Not since the San Francisco earthquake of 1906 had an American city been so ravaged. Destruction was visited equally upon dowager and draftsman, psychiatrist and janitor, Negro, white, and Mexican.

SEARCH AND CONVERGENCE

The storm's victims, emerging like moles into the fading sunlight, faced the task of putting together a traumatically shattered world. The initial concern was for family and close friends:

> The first thing I thought of was my fiance—I just got engaged last Saturday. I was in quite a daze. And one girl came up and said, "May I help you," and I said, "Well, I can't find my fiance." And I started running and looking.

Often at considerable personal risk, people wandered through broken glass and rubble in an attempt to locate relatives. One woman's relatives "walked through seven blocks of live wires and tree limbs to find that my house was practically kindling . . . then they went from hospital to hospital."

As night settled over the twisted wreckage and the sparking power lines, people came en masse to the disaster area. Reported one of the victims, "Cars were lined up for a block and people exchanged observations and feelings." Many of those who converged on the wreckage were looking for family and friends. Said the police chief:

> It is difficult to hold back anyone who is searching for his daughter. I don't think they've ever passed laws that say what you can do with human behavior in the time of disaster. We have been asking people to come to the aid of their fellow men for many many years now. I don't think it was any time for us to tell the people we didn't need their services.

However, the crowds were not all looking for friends and kin. Relative strangers offered help. It was not uncommon for people emerging from the rubble of their home to encounter unknown people who offered shelter and food for the night. A service station manager reported that:

Customers came from miles away to help. I had one boy, Pete, come from clear across town to help pick up the rubble and move things around. He really made me feel good.

On the other hand, a few looters were active. Reported one volunteer worker:

A group of teenage boys were about to carry off an electric drill and some other tools that had been scattered in the rubble. "Is this your house?" I asked one of them. He didn't say anything. "Are these your tools?" No answer. I said, "Put those things down and get your asses out of here." I realized suddenly that I was shouting and that my legs were beginning to tremble. The boys looked surprised, put down the tools, and left in a hurry.

But the largest group of people appeared to be drawn by simple curiosity. The tornado was important, it was exciting, it was a landmark event. They wanted to see and experience what had occurred:

It seemed that everyone in Topeka was going out toward the southwest part of town. When we got out on the highway three lanes were almost blocked: full of cars that were stopped and people were out taking pictures and looking at the wreckage.

They were, in effect, tourists of disaster.

The sightseers and helpers posed a major problem to the rescue crews. At 8:15 Bill Kurtis was pleading on WIBW:

Please do not go out into the streets. News reporters report the traffic is very congested and the ambulances are just barely able to get into Twenty-ninth and Gage, the most heavily damaged part of town. There are injuries and the ambulances must get through! *Please* do not go out, even though the all clear has sounded for the immediate Topeka vicinity.

Such requests did little good; the area was soon inundated.

This kind of mass convergence on disaster is an oft-reported phenomenon. Fritz and Williams (1957, p. 46) speak of the consequences in most disasters, echoing in a larger scale the concerns of Bill Kurtis:

> Within minutes following most domestic disasters, thousands of persons begin to converge on the disaster area and on first aid stations, hospitals, relief, and communication centers in the disaster environs. . . . The movement of emergency vehicles is often blocked by severe traffic congestion; essential outgoing messages are frequently delayed as a result of the heavy volume of incoming inquiries and messages; and the tons of unsolicited goods, in large proportion comprised of unneeded and unusable materials, greatly contribute to traffic congestion and require personnel and facilities and handling and storage which could be used for more essential tasks and functions.

Yet it is hard to know whether this mass inundation of the stricken area is more harmful or helpful. Much emergency help —both psychological and material—became immediately available as people converged like white cells around the city's wounds.[1]

[1] Reports of post-disaster activity disagree markedly on whether such activities are functional or dysfunctional. Fritz and Marks (1954, p. 33), for example, observed "a very considerable amount of confused and uncoordinated activity during and following almost all the disasters studied by us." Baskt, Berg, Foster, and Raker (1953, p. 58) agree, viewing the volunteer response as "undisciplined," and recommending that "planning for future disaster must assume that this response is to be controlled and channeled in the proper directions." Other investigators, however, highlight the functional aspects of reactions to disaster. Killian (1954, p. 68) describes disaster activity which may give the "appearance of disorganized personal behavior," but is actually adaptive "structuring activity." The disaster actor seeking "normative orientation," according to Demerath (1957, p. 28), often violates the "usual social expectations" which he now perceives to be inappropriate, and "in terms of the new situation, his behavior may be altogether rational." Form and Nosow (1958, p. 24) suggest that post-disaster behavior be understood "as the functioning of relatively complex systems of social relationships" having the result of "maintaining recognizable social ties." Individually improvised disaster activity, "with all the confusion and lack of coordination involved," may be necessary, states Barton (1962, p. 223), if community formal organizations cannot cope with the effects of the calamity. "Behavior during a disaster which is functional for one group," advise Deutscher and Kongming New (1957, p. 34), "may be perceived as dysfunctional by other groups involved."

DAZE

In the chaos of the evening, the victims began to reunite with family and friends. The immediate response of the victims was similar—not panic, not even excitement, but rather a reaction of daze. Many accounts of this dazed state were given:

> It was a strange, real strange feeling. A real unhealthy calm. People just wandered up and down, kind of like nobody knew what happened and nobody knew what to do. They didn't talk about the tornado; they didn't talk about their house. They all needed to go somewhere but they did not know where to go. We were kind of looking around. We couldn't mobilize ourselves to do anything. This lasted for several days. We would meet in the hall and there would be conversations—What are you going to do? Where are you going? Are you going to stay where you are? And nobody was doing anything except sort of staring inside their apartment.

This is a subjective account. Observers saw the victims as detached, zombie-like. One woman observed of a friend:

> She wasn't her usual capable self. She was really removed from reality of the whole thing. It was as if she were in a dream. The family itself were like lost souls and they wandered about; their chief concern seemed to be to see which of their belongings were unscathed. It was dreamlike.

Coupled with the daze was gratitude, and a sense of wonder at one's own safety amidst the wreckage. As reports came in from search crews and hospitals, the city discovered in amazement that relatively few people had been injured, and fewer yet killed. The 1953 Waco, Texas, tornado, which had been less physically destructive, had killed 356; in Topeka 17 died. In the next few days one heard the same comment repeated from many lips: "It was a miracle."

For Topeka, the night of June 8 began in tranquillity; it

ended in shock and anguish. At midnight dazed victims were still being reunited with family and friends; hastily mobilized rescue crews were digging through rubble; the police, Air Force, and National Guard were setting up road blocks; volunteer groups were congregating in schools and churches to provide emergency aid. And from everywhere people came to experience this strange disruption of their expectable world, swarming into the disaster area like so many ants when the ant hill has been shattered by the unthinking boot of a hiker.

This then was the disaster: sudden, overwhelming, dramatic. Like war or the death of a president, it served as a landmark in the lives of all who experienced it. For the newspaper readers and television viewers in other cities, the tornado itself was the central event; it and the resultant human anguish were imbibed along with the morning coffee and corn flakes, arousing a momentary flash of sympathy and concern, and then in a few days forgotten. Not so for Topeka. For Topeka the actual, concrete disaster was only the beginning of a much longer process of adaptation and recovery. Just as the story of World War II is not told by Pearl Harbor, neither is the story of the tornado told by the initial crisis. It is in the painful unfolding of later events that the true drama lies.

Perhaps the best image is this: the tornado quite literally set the stage. It changed and disrupted the physical world. People found themselves cast precipitously into new roles. Unexpectedly they confronted new demands, both individual and social. They reacted in new ways, and their reactions led to new forms of social functioning. For a period after the disaster, ordinary cares and concerns seemed to be laid aside. The city was caught up in a collective excitement and a profound sense of shared destiny, wherein the fate of one's neighbor was as important as one's own. The result, for a brief moment, was a kind of community coherence seldom encountered outside of war, or the transcendental states of mass religious excitement. For a while the city became a different organism and functioned by different rules. It is this newness, this ephemeral process of adaptation and recovery, which forms the topic of the following chapters.

We shall begin, as did the citizens of Topeka when the storm had passed, by focusing upon the pivotal actors of the drama—the tornado victims.

CHAPTER TWO

VICTIMS

O F ALL THE PEOPLE involved in disaster, it is the victim who stands out most clearly. The very word, "victim," conjures up stereotypes: the child wandering through rubble, the family dispossessed, the mass of homeless people huddled in emergency shelters. The victim is a figure of sympathy, a person to be helped. The mass media reflect this stereotype; it is common after disaster to read of the courage, fortitude, endurance, and gratitude displayed by victims. Few indeed are the stories of shiftless victims, ill-tempered victims, cowardly victims, or the victim as ingrate. This is a bit odd, since calamity and trauma do not automatically lead people to become paragons of virtue. Is there something special about disaster, something which enhances the nobility of all victims? Or is it that the norms of society cause us to look at victims in a special way? Is it possible that the victims are cast into, and come to accept and play, a special role? Perhaps being a "victim" is more complicated than appears on the surface.

A second kind of complication emerges as we look at the psychological effects of the storm and its aftermath. We have already indicated some of these complexities in Chapter 1, in discussing the issues of disbelief and daze. Being a victim is a psychological as well as a social matter. The psychology of the victim-state merits analysis, both for its own sake and for an understanding of its social consequences.

In this chapter, then, we shall explore this matter of being a victim, looking at both its psychological and its social elements. From the psychological side, we shall examine the motivational mechanisms which underlay different kinds of reaction, focusing especially on the zombie-like "disaster syndrome," on the rarer syndrome of disaster elation, and on the stoic response. From the social side, we shall examine "being a victim" as an ephemeral social role with its own particular attributes, expectations, and stresses. We shall start, however, not with such abstract issues but with the raw phenomena of experience.

TWO VICTIMS

The first victim is a professional man, forty-eight years old, whose family was attending a concert on Washburn campus:

> We saw the sky with the debris swirling around, and realized that this was a tornado. Somebody yelled, "Get down everybody," and we lay down on the floor. My wife was near me, and she grabbed my daughter and lay on top of her. People tried to get under the seats. They didn't seem to be much protection. Most of us just lay on the ground in the open room.

And the whole thing at that point went very fast. I didn't hear any noise, nor did some of the others. But within what seemed to be a matter of moments it was over, and there was just a feeling that dust was settling on everything. A kind of gray dust had fallen and covered us; it had been shaken either from the ceiling or had blown in through the window. We realized there had been a storm and it had passed.

Everybody was getting up and asking who was hurt, and most people weren't. A couple of us decided to go out into the hallway, and when we got to the door it was completely blocked. We pushed against it, but there was no budging it. We realized something in the building had fallen in and we were blocked in the room. Then we looked at the window and saw we could climb out.

And through the whole thing there was very little awareness of the seriousness of what had happened overhead.

We began to help people through the shattered window and into the rubble. And even then we did not have a real comprehension of the extent of the damage. There were downed power lines every place, and we were aware of this as a danger, and the needing to shepherd the kids. We had to climb over rocks.

The informant reported to a relief center. There he found himself, for the first time, cast in the role of the victim:

It was odd. The place was divided into those who were victims, and those who were there to help—the helpers couldn't quite believe that something dreadful had happened, except that they were seeing the evidence in the people. I had this odd state of not quite knowing to which group I belonged. You know, we didn't realize what a close call we had. We saw it as inconvenience, and of course the loss of a car, and were saying that we were lucky that none of us were hurt. Yet we didn't feel the emotional impact of how lucky we were or how badly hurt financially so many others were.

Typically, the informant was not aware of any appearance of daze in himself:

> I wasn't aware of feeling anything like it myself, but people felt that I was. I was aware of an inadequate comprehension of the extent of what we've been through. It was as if I were only partially aware of it. And it was as if I were minimizing the whole thing and feeling that, "Well, I've been through a slight inconvenience rather than a major threat to life." I heard in a roundabout way that somebody saw me when I was at the relief center that night, and remarked on how dazed and white I seemed to be. But I had no awareness of being different from what I usually am.

With a mounting realization of the past danger came a mounting sense of shock. The experience began to have a more total impact:

> We really had no idea until the next day. It was a kind of gradual dawning realization over several days—the extent of the damage, the devastation, the people killed, and the close call we had had.
>
> The first night our youngest daughter couldn't sleep well, awakened with nightmares a couple of times.
>
> The next day at work I was shaking a good deal, especially as a lot of people commented on what happened to us. And the more they commented on it, with a surprise how close our call had been, the more I had a kind of preoccupation and a kind of thinking back over it.
>
> I still have this reaction in a way, every time I happen to drive through any tornado area. It will be years before the scars will disappear. The stripped-bare trees make it look desolate, you know, like a moon-type landscape.

In this account are several issues to which we shall return again. The quickness of the tornado—its unreality and unexpectedness—had its psychological implications. After the tornado the victims faced the task of dealing with a new social reality. First, there was the task of checking on family and friends; second, a need to find shelter and help; and third, the task of revising future plans. But more than this, the people caught up in disaster faced another issue: they were willy-nilly cast into a specific role—the role of the victim. Here again was an event which had its own psychological implications.

By way of contrast, consider a second person caught in the tornado path. This is a middle-aged, widowed, professional woman who had lived fifteen years in an apartment which on the night of June 8 was totally destroyed:

> The first thing I knew of the tornado was the roar. I heard no sirens; my apartment was closed up except for an open window in the bedroom. I did hear the roar and the lights went out, so I rushed over to get out of the apartment. I had been under a tornado before and I knew the sound. The only window near me was in the bathroom. Everything outside was flying around in an odd motion. I shall never forget it. I was on my way to the door; then I couldn't get the door open. I didn't think about dying or anything else. I was just frightened.
>
> And then my ceiling crashed. And I kept tugging at this door, and I couldn't open it. Finally I got down in front of the door. I don't think people think very well. I just did it, getting down in front of it. I waited a little bit, tried the door again, and it opened. In front of me was all kinds of stuff hanging down from the ceiling. And I crawled under it, and over a bunch of other stuff, and went to the basement. By that time it was over. The people there looked at me sort of strangely, and they said, "It's over." And we went upstairs.
>
> Outdoors it was awful, because everybody was out there and just staring. People would stand there and say, "I have nowhere to live!" But they did; many had adult children they could stay with. One woman had a very devoted son, and yet she said, "He can't take me in." Mostly people just stood and looked at our trees, and made lots of comments about our gorgeous trees that weren't there any more. None of us looked at our apartments to see what the damage was.

I don't know what we saw, except our trees and each other.

There were lots of live wires and all kinds of stuff—the smell of gas—and we were aware of these things. And somebody would say "Watch out!" It was very peculiar!

Everybody was showing a real unhealthy calm. Just kind of looking. People just wandered up and down. They didn't talk about the tornado, they didn't talk about their apartment.

A lot of people were saying they had no place to go. Several people said this to me, and I would argue with them: "What about so-and-so?" For instance, Dr. White's mother-in-law was there, and she said, "I haven't any place to go." I said, "What about Dick?" And she said, "Oh no, Dick can't take care of me."

For two days the informant stayed at the apartment of her relative:

I didn't sleep. I couldn't do anything the next day. I put a telephone call through to my daughter in Arizona. But I was in a state of shock for most of this time. I went over to my apartment twice, but I could not mobilize myself to do anything. Everybody there simply looked. We would meet out in the hall of the ruined building and there would be conversation: not about the terrible tornado, but sort of "What are you going to do? Where are we going? Are you going to stay where you are?"—this sort of thing. And nobody was doing anything except staring inside their apartment.

Later, I think we were forcing ourselves every step of the way. We would work and we would sit down. I felt like crying some: I didn't, but I felt like it.

It was awfully easy not to work. I said once that I wished it had blown everything I had away. Then I wouldn't have so much to decide: Does this go into storage? Does this go with me? Will I need this? Where am I going to be permanently? These easy decisions are hard, because you don't know where you are going, and you don't know what you are going to want.

I found this a very horrible experience, and it got worse for me. And then it had to rain! When I came back it was the biggest mess I ever saw: The ceiling had fallen, and all my things were water-soaked. Everything had water all over it. Some people came along to help, and they spent about thirty minutes with me, because when they would pick up a carton the bottom would fall out. Then they had to pick up all the stuff and pack it up again.

I left and went to my niece's, and I said, "I'm through. I quit." And she didn't say anything, but just disappeared and came back with some cartons. She said, "Come on." So we went back and took all that water-soaked stuff.

I continued to feel bad: My worst day was Sunday [June 12]. I could hardly keep from crying. Of course, I was physically tired. I think everyone was terribly tired, and I don't think anyone slept very much. For no reason at all tears would come to my eyes. So I went back to work.

Now when I go back and look around all the familiar things are gone—the house and a tree. You get the feeling that you're in a foreign city, because nothing is familiar.

And I wonder why none of us can stay away from where we lived. I went out Sunday, and I looked it all over again. I saw the caretaker out there today and I said, "I'm just like a criminal who goes back to his crime. I go out here all the time." And she said, "We all do. All the people who lived here come back all the time."

It's a miserable experience! Don't let it ever happen to you—if you can help it!

In this account is seen a different reaction to the disaster—depression rather than anxiety. The focus is more upon a sense of loss; regaining composure took more time. The grim task of recovery added another burden, and it is hinted that "being a victim" sometimes clashed with other, deeply held values—that sometimes people were reluctant to ask for help, or lose their independence.

One way of looking at, and comparing, the reactions of the

victim group is to define the tasks which confronted them at different stages of the tornado. As the above accounts suggest, and as our other interviews made clear, it is possible to think of four different groups of issues or tasks which confronted the victims. These are: (1) dealing with the immediate onslaught and aftermath of the tornado and the feelings it aroused; (2) dealing with the new role and role expectations of being a "victim"; (3) developing plans for recovery and putting them into action; and (4) dealing with the aftereffects of the tornado and with residual feelings. These tasks occur in stages over time; we shall examine each of them in turn.

DISBELIEF, DISRUPTION, REINTEGRATION

Most of us, in our day-to-day activities, operate within a stable and expectable environment. There is a smooth continuity between one moment and the next, and within the physical landscape through which we move. For the victim, the tornado abruptly disrupted this continuous and predictable life. Suddenly, unexpectedly, it occurred; and the safe and comfortable world vanished in an instant. It was the suddenness of the experience which forcibly struck many of our respondents:

> It happens too quick for you to comprehend at that moment. It just seems like it's—well, maybe you're looking at a picture. It doesn't touch you personally. It isn't real to you. It is more a feeling of disbelief, kind of like a bad dream.

It was, in fact, so quick that many people were only aware of random and diffuse thoughts: important aspects of the experience were not noted until later:

> Pow! Down came the whole fireplace and chimney all in one piece. It glanced off the end of the piano, and I heard the legs go crack crack! I felt a little bit of panic in the pit of my stomach, and I thought, "The legs are going to give way, and we will have the piano on top of us." But it only

takes a minute 'til you realize they've held, so the panic subsides.

The whole chimney fell in and caught just the sole of my shoe, and I didn't even realize I was caught until I tried to get out. It caught Alice across the legs, and she said, "Oh my legs!" and moaned. Or maybe that was later.

Afterward I noticed that my hair was full of mud balls, plaster, splinters, and everything. There was so much plaster dust that I was choking, and I felt this rising panic in the pit of my stomach again. "Will I smother?" But I coughed, and afterward realized that I was going to survive it. The panic went down. Then as it began to calm I could hear above me the noise of the gas, and again that panic: gas! And then the realization: we're in open air, we're not going to be asphyxiated if someone doesn't light a match. So then all of a sudden it was quiet.

During the abrupt crisis of the tornado, some things were noticed, but much was disregarded. Feelings of fear arose, then subsided:

You could hear very large crashes of things coming down, and above it a constant breaking of glass. I suddenly had the realization and the anxiety of someone not just being scratched, but really getting injured seriously. Just as I felt myself coming to grips with this, it was over.

The quickness of the onslaught made it difficult to integrate the experience with all that had preceded it. When it came, the tornado happened so quickly that it was impossible to form a gestalt, or to be aware of it as a totality. The task of integrating the new experience with the old was therefore not accomplished during the crisis, but only later. It was like the common experience of the combat soldier, who may discover that he is wounded only when he is out of battle. It is therefore not surprising that most reported reactions to the tornado were concerned not with the experience itself, but with its immediate aftermath. The following account is typical:

There was a barely perceptible let-up and I opened my eyes. Bright daylight! All my wife and I could do was to exchange glances. I spoke first: "Honey, we lost everything, but thank God we're alive!" Everyone in our room was alive. The four of us worked our way around to the front of what had been our apartment. Boards, ripped panels, torn clothing were strewn everywhere. There wasn't a single wall standing. In the darkened twilight, the only familiar object was a little refrigerator, which was cocked at a forty-five-degree angle.

The immediate task was to find a familiar landmark, a point of beginning. Something had to be done, but what? I felt an inner gratitude that the family was together and alive. The gathering darkness heightened the sense of desolation and destruction.

Time and again we heard of this sequence: the thankfulness for survival, the immediate concern about one's family, and the attempt to reorient the self in a changed and unfamiliar world.

The source of disruption and confusion thus lay in the quickness of the onslaught, the lack of time for psychological preparation. But a second factor was important as well. This was the loss of a stable world. The sudden disruption of the landscape—the barren world as scarred as a bombed out city—had profound implications for many:

It became impossible to absorb. You see all these trees down, and buildings down, and you can't absorb it or talk about it. Then slowly, by picking out one little facet at a time, you can start talking. We saw people straggling out of the ruined Washburn Chapel. I did not realize that any of them had been trapped. This is a strange kind of phenomena. You see a buliding which has been torn apart, and you see people coming out of it dazed, and somehow the association of *these* people having been in *that* building doesn't seem to take place. It has a strange kind of split to it . . . it doesn't make sense—it's only when you can back away from it a little bit that the image forms of people sitting in a room, and being pelted by plaster as it falls down on them.

Not only was it hard to integrate experience in this strange and unexpected world, but the abrupt loss of expectable landscape at times produced a more profound disorganization. One minister, walking through a low-income area of the city immediately after the tornado, reported of a parishioner:

> The mother of the house was all right as long as she stayed in the bedroom. She seemed to be well collected there, because the bedroom still seemed like home and didn't have any kind of serious damage. But the minute she walked out into the main part of the house where she could see the roof was gone, she would get all upset. Her sister was making every effort she could to keep her in the bedroom through the night. She was hoping to get her oriented the next day.

The loss was emotional as well as cognitive: a landscape full of warm and human meanings had gone. A young office worker reported her feelings as she passed her ruined apartment house:

> It still sort of shakes me up; it's just so amazing. And the feeling of comfort I remember always when coming home at night; you always see big lights up in those pretty apartments, and this was home. And then all of a sudden it's dark and there is nothing there, and it's still a little unbelievable.

Loss of landscape, then, meant not just loss of predictable environment, but also partial loss of environmental supports and rituals which give life meaning.

Especially poignant were those losses which tied the person to his past. An aspiring writer typed out his impressions:

> We passed the Washburn Campus. I have studied here, and I sat against these tree stubs, walked in the buildings, and now it's all gone and I feel emptied, as though what had happened here, what I had learned, is gone too. Part

of the ethos of any university is its permanence, the fact that however modern or small or large it may be, whatever its physical manifestation, part of its function is to compress Time, to encapsulate it for the consumption of people who work and study there. And now this place can't do that anymore. For the first time I feel that a part of my own life has been affected by the tornado.

Part of the poignancy of the experience lay in the contrast effect. The tornado area was devastated and grim, but one could walk a few blocks and find a city going about its usual business in its customary way:

I have the truck drop me off at the edge of Westboro, where I am to have dinner with friends. And as I walk into Westboro I have as great a sense of disorientation, of unreality, as anything I've experienced all day. Here the lawns are carefully manicured, birds are singing in the confident stately trees, children are laughing, discreetly it seems, and I envy them. A woman is talking with her gardener about begonias, in a quiet voice, but it is so peaceful here that I can hear every word of the conversation as I walk by the house. It would appear that all was not well with the begonias. I am dead tired, the contrasts of the day have been so great that I feel I've gone from one side of the moon to the other —but where is the earth?

In a sense, then, the loss of personal landscape can be seen as producing disorientation, not only because it disrupted the predictable world of the present, but because it symbolized a loss of the past. Certain of our more sophisticated informants commented upon a loss of identity. One, for instance, noted his great relief at finding his wallet: the identity cards provided him a symbolic base from which to start. By contrast, his wife, who had borne up well throughout the disaster period, broke into tears when she discovered that her pocketbook was missing: "So much in it reinforced her identity—her lipstick and all the other

things that women carry in their pocketbook to comfort them—
and it was all gone."

The loss of a personal landscape was only one psychological
stress imposed by the storm. Another lay in the meaning of the
storm itself; an erratic, overwhelming, and impersonal force:

> I think this made a lot of people take stock. They are
> not as powerful as their fantasies would lead them to be-
> lieve. I heard this from many people. It's pretty stupid to
> be thinking that you are all powerful and your houses are
> that strong.

DAZE AND THE "DISASTER SYNDROME"

In the face of this flood of problems and feelings, the individual struggled to maintain a sense of self-control. Different
people did this in different ways: one victim wrote an account
of his feelings as he asked a friend for help:

> I stood in mud-splattered slacks, my boy wrapped in a
> green blanket in my arms. The most disconcerting aspect,
> however, was that I seemed more composed than my friend.
> He invited me in and then ran to the basement stairs yelling
> for his wife. I felt a little self-conscious—a refugee on dis-
> play. I disliked any semblance of lack of control. It re-
> minded me of my own uncertainty and vulnerability, which
> I did not want to acknowledge or display. At this point I
> guess I had only two things. I had my self-control, and I
> had to maintain it. I did this through humor and appearing
> nonchalant. I acted as if I had misplaced a handkerchief,
> not that my home had blown away! And I also had my boy.
> My friends offered to hold him or put him to bed. But I
> wouldn't let him go—not for the world. I justified this by
> saying he would be too upset if he left me. Maybe it was
> the other way around. But we had lost so much I wasn't
> going to take a chance for him.
>
> I tried to make conversation as a way of avoiding my
> own silent thoughts. I voiced my bewilderment over what

plans to make for the future, knowing this was hardly an appropriate subject for the present moment. Then I compared the destruction to a bombed-out city: "This should make me a confirmed pacifist," I remarked. I just had to demonstrate my self-control.

Many of our informants noted a dazed reaction among the immediate victims. Other reports indicate this to be a common response—so common that Wallace (1956, p. 125) has labeled it "the disaster syndrome." He describes the state as follows: ". . . [the] injured and uninjured are 'dazed,' 'apathetic,' 'stunned'; awareness of the extent and intensity of destruction to person, family, and community is inadequate; . . . many people simply stare, wander aimlessly, 'putter about'; expressions of strong emotion (grief, fear, pain, anger, etc.) are missing or sporadic and unimportant."

Tyhurst (1951, p. 766), reporting on field surveys of four disasters, estimates that the large majority of the victims—perhaps three-fourths—were "stunned and bewildered . . . show-[ing] . . . a definite restriction of the field of attention; lack of awareness of any subjective feeling or emotion although manifesting the physiological concomitants of fear. . . ." Such diverse accounts, coming from a wide variety of disasters, suggest that a general psychological mechanism is at work.

How can this reaction, the "disaster syndrome," be understood? Two processes seemed especially important. In the first place, the victims had recently escaped from a sudden and dangerous situation; with a realization of the danger came a physiological reaction and a sense of shock. Some of the energy used to deal with the external reality was turned inward, directed toward handling the many feelings aroused by the trauma. Second, the victim found himself in a totally unpredicted and confusing situation: a situation in which personal expectations were fragmented and destroyed. He somehow had to deal with the new situation and master it. The process of reintegration took energy too. In psychoanalytic terms, attention cathexes were withdrawn from the external world in order to defend against the internal on-slaught of disruptive affect, and to serve the needs of reintegra-tion and working through. The result, to the observer, was the robot-like behavior, the "going through the motions," of the dazed state.

In part, our view of the disaster syndrome is similar to that of Wallace (1957, p. 26) who points to the importance of per-ceptual disruption in producing the dazed state. He suggests an analogy between the predictable social world and a maze through which individuals have learned to move to achieve expectable rewards. By this analogy, the maze of the environment presents the individual with learned cues for behavior, just as the white rat learns to respond to cues as he threads his way through the maze to a food pellet. Disaster produces a "sudden physical de-struction of the maze itself, or a part of it." The dazed reaction is a response to "maze-way disintegration"; the individual is cue-less and lost. Allowing for differences in terminology, the basic no-tion of "maze-way disintegration" clearly implies the task of perceptual restructuring which our interviews so emphasize.[1]

Wolfenstein (1957, p. 79) emphasizes more the task of affect control: ". . . the disaster victim has been forced to take in more than he can for the moment assimilate, his energies be-come engrossed in the task of mastering, of gradually inuring himself to the sudden and terrible experience." This process she sees as the major source of the dazed reaction.

In common with many psychologically sophisticated theo-rists, Wolfenstein (p. 80) tries to relate the disaster syndrome to other pathological states, in this case, the syndrome of depression.

---

[1] These observations are pertinent to an issue of general import for psycho-logical theory: that is, the role played by perceptual input in the maintenance of adequate ego functioning. Our observations suggest that a sudden disruption of perceptual expectations has a profound cognitive and affective impact, and is central to the understanding of the disaster syndrome. The experimental studies of stimulus distortion support this suggestion. It has been generally found that perceptual distortion or deprivation arouses marked anxiety (Hebb, 1958; Kub-zansky and Landerman, 1961). The theoretical implications of such findings are discussed from a psychoanalytic point of view by Rapaport (1958).

The victims, she says, are emotionally dull and unresponsive, and show a marked inhibition of activity. These reactions reflect a sense of abandonment and loss of omnipotence. She suggests that the victim may also view the disaster as punishment. "All these factors," she claims, "are destructive of the individual's self-esteem. There is the feeling: I cannot be much good if this could happen to me; I am not omnipotent, nor lovable, nor virtuous."

Although our interviews suggest that the victim does indeed struggle to control his feelings, our findings give no support to the idea that "daze" is related to pathological depression. A sense of loss was common, and mourning too, but none of the informants and none of the psychotherapy cases reported that they felt punished or blame-worthy. Self-esteem never reached the level of self-denigration typical of depression, nor was there much sense of being singled out for special punishment. Perhaps the crucial difference is contained in the phrase "singled out." A solitary individual afflicted by misfortune may suspect that he is being punished by a righteous God for his sins. But when disaster uniformly strikes a heterogeneous mass of people, the event is less likely to be seen in such personal terms.

A related view sees the "disaster syndrome" as a manifestation of "psychological stress." Thus, K. A. Menninger (1954, p. 285) suggests that major stress may push the individual into increasingly dysfunctional modes of adaptation, the second stage being *"characterized by partial detachment from the world of reality."* The "disaster syndrome" would seem to reflect such "partial detachment." Engel (1962, p. 282) similarly differentiates two modes of response to psychological stress: anxiety and depression-withdrawal. He sees the disaster victim as showing "many of the characteristics of the primitive depression withdrawal reaction." This is not to claim that such stress behavior is a result of physiological reactions. Engel, for instance, defines psychological stress as "all processes, whether originating within the environment or within the person, which impose a *demand* or *requirement* upon the organism, *the resolution or handling of which requires work or activity of the mental apparatus* before any other system is involved or activated (p. 264; italics added). "Stress response" thus becomes synonymous with adaptation. To understand the disaster syndrome as a particular stress response, it is necessary to understand the specific demands imposed by disastrous events and the most likely adaptation to these demands. We have tried to provide such understanding in the preceding pages.[2]

In brief, daze may be viewed as a form of adaptation. But "daze" was not the only reaction to the tornado. Some victims felt a sense of elation. They appeared excited, laughing, hyperactive. The underlying mood here seemed to be, "Look Ma, it missed me!"

As soon as I got to safety I became very hyper, and I talked a lot. I was a little shaky, and a little sick to my stomach, but really all right. It's just that I felt I wasn't quite with it. Shook up, I guess, would be a better way to describe it. I was excited, and I felt elated—the elation of being alive. The only thing I cared about was that I found my engagement ring. I had been upset about losing it, and I was sure that I would never find it in all of the junk from the tornado. And I didn't think about anything else that I had lost, even though I knew that I had lost everything. But even before then I thought, "Oh, but at least we are all right, and I have my fiance, and that's the important thing." I felt good. Very relieved and elated. You know, it even got to the point where we were joking around a little bit, just like three girls sitting and having an evening together eating sandwiches and having a drink while we watched TV.

[2] A brief review of the varying definitions of "psychological stress" is given by Janis (1958, pp. 11–13). Although the notion of "stress" as an explanatory variable is complicated by conceptual problems, most definitions of the construct imply some sort of stimulus change (stress or threat) which arouses unpleasant affect, and leads to adaptive attempts—variously conceived as re-establishment of homeostasis (K. A. Menninger, 1954), or coping behavior (Hermann, 1965), or the like.

Implicit in this elation is a claim for omnipotence: "I am not a victim in the face of the storm. I have escaped death; I am guarded from damage." As in any attempt to deny human vulnerability, this mood may be shaken by intrusive reality. For the woman quoted above, it was noteworthy that the elation was followed by tearfulness and depression.

Three psychotherapy cases who showed exhilaration also expressed a sense of being especially favored. One therapist saw the elation as coming from "being so close to violent destruction, so close and not yet being a primary victim. There's some kind of excitement in having an experience with such tremendous destructiveness." Another therapist remarked of a case, "Some magic qualities came into it. She had a feeling that something looked out for her even in the face of all this. It was as though she had gone through something and had been untouched by it." Perhaps notable too is the fact that all three psychotherapy cases were women, and all three enjoyed the gratification of dependency needs which came about with the offers of help and succor in the wake of the tornado. Such gratifications too could be seen as a fulfillment of omnipotence fantasies.

Besides elation and daze, a third reaction—stoic calm—was occasionally found. The psychotherapists reported several victims who reacted this way to the tornado's onslaught. The stoics simply went about their necessary business in a stolid and unemotional fashion. One such case is described by a therapist:

> He is an extremely intelligent professional man, extremely methodical in his thinking. Isolation and reaction formation are very much a part of his character. No great emotionalism, almost at any time. When he heard on the radio the tornado was coming he went around the house methodically. He opened the doors and windows. This is typical; he's too self-controlled for his own good. The analysis would go a lot faster if he could loosen up. He's got almost an ironclad obsessive-compulsive defense system. His dream imagery indicates the nature of his defenses. He dreamed of

a steel railroad car—no, a steel vault—and what was inside
was anger.

Another case, ostensibly much different, was described in similar
terms:

> I have one patient who is twenty-one years old. She
> wasn't at home at the time the tornado hit but was visiting
> somewhere. She was surprisingly calm about the tornado,
> as if her own personal problems and what her therapist was
> going to do overshadowed all this. It was a mundane report-
> ing of the mess—no great loss over what she had.
>
> This girl has been put in the position of being the head
> of the family, even though she is not even the oldest child.
> Her parents seem incapable of functioning very well them-
> selves. Each parent relies on her for guidance, even though
> she is only twenty-one years old. There have been no torna-
> does before, but in the other family storms everybody just
> looks to her to be the Rock of Gibraltar and take it in stride.
> This is part of it, and part of it comes from her apprehension
> about not really permitting herself to express how she really
> feels. The storm was so repressed that she didn't permit
> herself to feel the loss, the danger, all the tragedy associated
> with it.

In short, this patient too maintained an equilibrium only by
keeping her defenses erect and strong; she could allow none of
the feelings to come through.

The same rigid defenses are apparent in a third case, but
for this patient the storm was in some sense disruptive:

> She was momentarily shaken and very frightened dur-
> ing the storm. But afterward when she looked out she was
> startled, but that was about it. She wasn't dazed. I think
> the next day she was more upset that her schedule had been
> interrupted.
>
> She is a girl who was reared very strictly, one of those
> difficult textbook cases whose parents always were giving her
> enemas and purgatives. The impressive thing all during our

work with her has been the degree of isolation and denial she shows. She goes in a straight line according to her motto, "First we do this, then we do that." There is a lot of the rigidity of the compulsive about her. Her reaction to the storm was consistent with the major trends in her personality. After it was over she preoccupied herself with salvaging what was salvagable and looking for a new apartment; she made endless difficulties there too. But as far as reacting to the fact—"I almost got killed"—this shook her only momentarily. It quickly got bound up into a network of ritual stuff.

It would appear, then, that the reaction of daze was a more direct response to the tornado than was the firm maintenance of stoic self-control. A matter-of-fact acceptance of the disaster seems in these few cases to arise from a too rigid defensive system, and from the need to impose self-controls no matter what the cost.

THE VICTIM ROLE

The tornado produced an elementary social division within the city of Topeka: there were those who had been directly affected by it, and those who had been untouched. As with all social divisions, the mere fact of difference produced expectations and stereotypes. For some, the world came to consist of victims and nonvictims. The victim found his house and possessions damaged, his life disrupted, his immediate future unclear. As a victim, he entered into a new series of transactions with others in the community: friends, volunteers, and agency helpers. Out of these transactions grew certain feelings and certain psychological demands. Part of the experience of being caught in a tornado lay in taking on this "victim role."

The elementary social split between victims and others quickly became apparent. An informant, whose house was leveled to the ground, describes an awareness of the social difference within half an hour after the tornado had passed:

Cars were already lined up for a block, and gathering groups exchanged observations and feelings. I immediately sensed an "over-againstness" quality: I was the participant, they were the spectators. My pride at being in the spotlight was qualified by the angry realization that my helplessness was exposed. They were talking about the tragedy, my family was experiencing it. Somehow I wanted to cut through them —to say "To hell with you"—and get my hands on a phone to call my friends.

To be a victim implied not only that the person had been touched by a unique event, but also that as a result he was helpless and needed succor. As the case-history material has already shown, the victimized person did not immediately accept this "victim role"; at first its implications were often denied. People "could not" ask their relatives to supply bed and board. In some cases, it was only when the relative appeared and clearly expected to give aid that the "victim role" was accepted.

DEPENDENCY AND AMBIVALENCE

Being in the dependent victim role was for some easy and for some hard. At times acceptance was notably ambivalent:

This morning people were talking about tornado victims, and this is something we all have difficulty accepting because we don't feel victimized. There is something very passive about being a victim. We neither feel victimized in the sense of passivity, nor do we feel that this was done to us. I can't remember hearing anywhere in the family any comments like, "Why did this happen to us?" There has never been this feeling.

As a matter of fact, both children expressed it—when the Red Cross canteen came around, they asked whether it would be all right for them to go to the canteen to get a coke or sandwich. Obviously the canteen was coming around for people who needed it. You know, we had to say to ourselves that we were in the class of people who need it. I would say we never really experienced the whole feeling of being a victim. I think we resorted to all kinds of dodges. These have the effect of saying, "No, we are not in that class." We don't talk about the tornado; we talk about the "storm."

Thus being a victim implied a dependence upon others which sometimes went against the grain. The same informant described it as a matter of family pride and competence:

> As a family we are not very comfortable with being waited on, or having other people do things for us. So while people were being enormously helpful around the house, their very helpfulness exerted a kind of pressure to do things that perhaps we would have postponed. You can't sit quietly by while somone is working and sweating and really going all out. You've got to work along with them.

Perhaps in response to this, many of the victims were shy about requesting help. A worker in the relief center noted that:

> I spent a brief time that evening with a pile of new blankets which Sears-Roebuck had contributed, and I was impressed by the fact that most people were tending to ask for minimum—with a family of six or eight, for instance, only two or three blankets would be requested.

This was a common response, but reactions varied widely:

> A Mexican family I knew absolutely refused any help at all because they wanted to be "unindebted"; others like our house guest and Mrs. H. found strength and gained independence from the security of knowing that someone cared.

In other words, reactions to the "victim role" depended in part upon one's desire for independence and autonomy. Perhaps because of these issues, most victims turned for help to family or close friends. Reciprocity was possible with them. One result was that most of the immediate needs were met, not by official agencies and "relief centers," but more directly by kith and kin. As a Red Cross volunteer explained:

Most people stay in their homes if they can, or stay with friends. They aren't going to stay in a mass shelter; it's too impersonal. You don't have the warmth of friends or the surroundings of a home.

Dependency in the face of a tornado is, however, different from ordinary dependency. The everyday norms of the society are clear: one should be independent and not lean on others. But in the aftermath of the tornado different norms apply: for the person in the victim's role, temporary dependency is allowed. Victims who wish to be dependent need not feel guilty. This occasionally happened. A psychotherapist said of a patient:

> Generally she tends more toward not letting people do things for her, even though she would like them to. But the tornado made it all right for her to be receptive to the people's gifts, and kind feelings, and hospitality. A lot of people were anxious to help—which she found quite agreeable. It was not at all hard for her to accept the offered help. As a matter of fact, she was letting other people do more for her than she had to. For instance, she was still staying at a friend's house a week later and enjoying this quite a bit. Yet you could see they were showing signs of this wearing thin. They were still cordial, but not quite as cordial as they had been. And so we talked about this, and I said, "Isn't this something of a signal that you may be enjoying this too much?" She was just eating it up—all this attention.

But quite apart from the feelings about being helpless, many victims indeed needed help. No matter how independent they wished to be, they had to accept aid. The result was sometimes a kind of transaction which we have labeled "role bargaining." The helpers would offer something; the victim would attempt to take less than was offered, or would somehow try to change the transaction. Consider one such case, for which only a report is available:

> He had to laugh about some of the things which happened. The helpers were so anxious to help and yet they

made for difficulties. The men who were trying to salvage
the things came from a farm background and had different
values than his. They would pull out some half-destroyed
article, and tell him, "If you take a hammer to that you can
fix it up okay"—and then they would put it on the truck.
The informant didn't want to discourage them because they
were being so helpful, but he was quite sure he would never
fix up the article. So, surreptitiously, after the helpers had
put it in the truck he would sneak up behind them and
throw it away again. They caught him at this late in the
afternoon, and he had a difficult time explaining what he
was up to. When they did finish loading up the truck at the
end of the day and moved everything to his new house, he
had to phone the Salvation Army so that he could give away
the useless junk.

Other victims would sometimes accept food with a feeling that
they were giving a favor to the eager helper.

Bargaining was not the only way of handling dependency.
At times the victims accepted help with private reservations; it
was possible to be amused at the helpers and their antics, and the
amusement took the sting away from dependency. A psychotherapist described the reactions of a middle-aged widow:

> She was quite pleased when her fellow workers from
> her office showed up. This gave her a sense of belonging to
> a group. And then she was a little amused when they showed
> up the second day to replace the plastic they'd put on; she
> thought they had done a good job the first time. This amount
> of attention amused her a little.
>
> And then when the Girl Scout troop came in at the same
> time the Red Cross cart was going down the street offering
> sandwiches and coffee to everybody, she began to laugh
> about it. And then around came somebody from the Method-
> ist Church, and somebody from the Christian Church, and
> she was in high humor—laughing quite a bit, telling me about
> all these people. Her laughter wasn't all positive. There was
> a little bit of laughing at these helping people who were

stumbling over each other. At the same time she took full advantage of all of them. She took the Red Cross sandwiches, and she went to the churches for hot meals, and she appreciated it, particularly the hot meal at night.

A contrary reaction, of course, is found among those who accepted the help angrily, as if the help were not being offered in the proper spirit, or as if not enough was being done. Thus, an informant in the low-income side of town commented:

> My main feeling was one of bitterness toward the volunteers, the people that were helping. I'm sure that they were full of the spirit of brotherhood and helping and sharing in time of need. I wondered though, what have they done for East Topeka so far? Would any of them work for fair housing? And where would they be later when the need for help goes on?

Or, in a less doctrinaire way:

> We had some people that came in to help us move the partitions out of the yard. They just wanted to help us out—a father and a son. I never saw them before: frankly, to be real honest, I think they were a little nosey. Probably this isn't the right attitude. But I think they were, although they helped us a great deal. I mean they worked hard enough, and we probably couldn't have gotten it cleaned up without their help.

THE FISH-BOWL EFFECT

Another, less benign aspect of the victim's role was apparent within two hours after the tornado. Every social category implies there are people who are part of an in-group—"us"—and others who are outsiders—"them." This division into "us" and "them" became apparent early. How else to understand the actions of photographers and sightseers who treated the victims sometimes as if they were, in the words of one annoyed informant, "animals in a zoo"?

People just wanted to see what the storm had done, and they swarmed in by the hundreds. They were really in your way when you wanted to get things done. People driving up and down the street, gawking. All of us were quite disgusted by the people who wanted to just walk around.

Very soon signs were up in front of a few ruined houses: "Gawk You Bastards," "Free Tour of the Tornado Area."

But it was not just observers with their cameras. People wandered on private property and through houses in which others still lived:

> As a matter of fact, your things seem to enter the public domain. The front door won't lock. You leave it closed but you come back and it's wide open, and apparently people have been through. Saturday I was over here all day sorting my things—old letters, bills, and personal letters. I sat out there all day Saturday under my pool umbrella and people took pictures as they went by.

> And then last night my brother said that twice yesterday he'd found the same woman scratching away in the ruins. She says she is looking for her own things, but nevertheless her behavior was so peculiar that we do not know whether she was really scavenging or perhaps just confused. Anyway, she was out on the front lawn today when he arrived, and he stopped and said, "What are you doing?" She said, "Just trying to find things from my house." He said, "But it isn't your house; it's my sister's house. I don't think you should be in here." And she just looked at the floor and went on scratching around. He did get her out of the house. She's the one who said, "Well, after all it's been condemned now." And then he went back later and found her there again.

> So he said, "Now come out! I told you to stay away from here! Your things couldn't possibly be here!" But she retorted, "Well, they are all in the public domain now!"

Given their own sense of uniqueness, and the actions of sightseers and camera bugs, the victims too sometimes felt as if they were personally in the public domain.

Within a surprisingly short period of time most of the victims seemed to have moved beyond from the immediate stress of the tornado. Reported one observer:

> There was an impenetrable, stoical, but funeral quality on Friday night, as if people were too numb and too paralyzed to make any real contact with each other. By Saturday evening and Sunday people had relaxed and were chatting, and beginning to smile. This capacity of so many people to mobilize their energies and focus them on finding solutions to desperately urgent problems impressed me over and over again.

The speed of remobilization appeared to vary in different sections of the city. In some it seemed rapid; in others, slow:

> In a low-income area there were repeated scenes of outside volunteers helping on salvage operations at a house where apparently able-bodied adults and teenagers were standing around not doing anything. Sometimes there was a strangely moving picture, of elderly people sitting on their porches rocking, watching the trucks and rescue workers go by, as if it were all a solemn parade.

Another observer reported of a low-income area:

> I'd say that first day there was very little morale at all. About a week later I talked to some of the people there, and they were going to rebuild and they had pretty high spirits about it. The wreckage was somewhat cleared away by then. By that time they'd recovered enough so they were looking forward to the challenge of getting back on their feet. They were joking about it—but I didn't hear any funnies that first night; there weren't any jokes then.

But in the beginning, immediately after the storm, the task of remobilization had seemed overwhelming everywhere. This was true for victims and helpers alike:

As I remember my reaction, I was almost immobilized by the enormity of the disaster. I felt overwhelmed by the devastated and bombed-out appearance of Washburn and the destruction of my friend's house. I was quite concerned about what I could do, but had no knowledge of any role that I could play.

Some people reacted initially by giving up:

I saw an elderly woman, in her eighties, sifting through her house. It was just about completely demolished. She was picking up one thing after another and dropping it. A member of her church came by and said, "You'd better leave here tonight. Do you have a place to stay?" She had a daughter across town. The church worker said, "Well, you'd better go." Her reaction was, "I can't leave all these things here." He said, "Well, take a half dozen of the important things. You really must leave."

She stood there and she picked up two or three things, and she looked at them, and then she dropped them and she said, "I'm ready. There is nothing here." And then she just walked away.

There were many stories of similar reactions, especially among the aged. Occasionally the volunteer helpers would find elderly people going about their business in a roofless house, unable to deal in any way with the task of reconstruction.

This feeling of being overwhelmed beyond all recourse generally disappeared in a few days. A number of the victims felt that remobilization was much helped by the human contact provided by helpers, both friends and strangers. Examples of this were given in Chapter 1; other reports stress it too. Help was especially important in aiding recovery from the dazed state immediately following the tornado:

Right after the tornado occurred we met a man who was standing in the foundation of his house. We asked him where he was during the storm. He pointed over to the corner of the house. There was nothing there. He seemed to be completely disoriented, and didn't know where he was going to go. We began to talk to him, so he moved away from the foundation and toward the street. He asked whether or not the Elder family was all right, and I told him that I thought they were—there was some wind damage but I didn't think anyone was hurt. We also told him there was temporary shelter at the Salvation Army. He said he wanted to stay where he was to guard the few valuables that remained. But he seemed very appreciative that we stopped to talk to him. It seemed to get him moving, and a little bit oriented to what had happened.

Noteworthy in this, as in most other contacts with helpers, was the immediate attempt of the helper to formulate plans. By focusing upon the immediate task—to move or not to move— the helpers seemed to offer hope for a manageable future. It was as if they were saying that futility was unnecessary. This message was important, since the sense of futility had to be overcome before any remobilization was possible.

But the development of plans did more. We have suggested earlier that the feeling of "daze" arose in part from the difficulty in integrating the tornado and its results into the ongoing stream of perception and cognition. The tornado abruptly shattered all future expectations. Help in remaking plans and in looking forward to a new future served an integrative function, so that the victim was able to remobilize. The process is spelled out in the following account by a friend of one victim:

> Her husband came back to the daily chores much faster than she did. She and the kids have been in a dreamlike state almost to the present. Sunday after the tornado they had a very low period. They didn't know whether it was all worth while—all this cleaning. Perhaps they would find out there was no future in it. Fortunately, the contractor came over that day. This was a turning point in their attitude. The contractor said that the house was structurally sound and could be rebuilt. It would take a lot of money but it would

all work out. They would have to sweat out a period of disorder and chaos but they could rebuild it.

Remobilization was often symbolized by small and at times defiant acts which said to the world, "We are not defeated." Sometimes people held parties atop the rubble:

> For the first three hours we were working like crazy. And then we got a little giddy. Dick crawled into the kitchen (which was a total loss) and opened up the refrigerator. Then he said, "Oh here's a six-pack of beer." It was still cold. And he said, "Let's all sit down and have a beer." He opened it and there were six beers, one for each of us. We found some old lawn chairs and we sat on them. I was sitting on this lawn chair, with a beer, smoking a cigarette and eating sandwiches. We started laughing and joking, and saying we were taking a break. And people would come picking through the rubble, from one apartment to the next.
>
> Of course there weren't any walls, so we would say, "Come in. We're having an open house. Sit down and relax before you faint." We really had a small party on top of the rubble.
>
> I remember thinking, "This is not appropriate." And there were people down below draining the pool, looking to see if anyone was dead or anything. Here they were doing this; it was a grim and horrible situation and I thought, "Well, people are gonna think we're just awful!" We were being disrespectful of the terrible disaster. But I think it was something we had to do.

Such parties were not uncommon, although seldom were they carried out in such dramatic setting. More usual is the following account:

> The few tenants that remained worked all day yesterday, sweeping and hosing the back area. Then last night they all got together for a hamburger party. There were about twenty people—it wasn't planned, but just a spontaneous situation. Everybody pulled together, somebody rounded

up some hamburger, somebody got the mustard, and somebody got the pickles. So the morale here and in other parts
of the city seems like one of a "fighting comeback." Nobody
is saying, "Lay down dear, we're gone!" It has been a
heartening feeling.

These parties were perhaps the most poignant example of solidarity and of symbolic renewal in the face of devastation. But
even the single act of cleaning a wall or clearing away debris
in the back yard sometimes had a symbolic meaning: as one
informant said, "The insurance company would have taken care
of it but we felt we had to do something."

The way these varying motivations, plans, and opportunities
came together into major decisions is exemplified in the following account of a man newly moved to a house near the university
campus:

The view across the campus isn't going to change; that
will be rebuilt. I could go up tomorrow and get a more satis-
fying house, and Topeka could be flooded out the day after
or another tornado could hit. You just can't buy a house
anywhere that is going to be guaranteed against these things.
On the negative side, one just doesn't walk away. People
talk about walking away from a house—I don't know what
the hell this means. In the first place you still owe the mortgage company the mortgage. There is always some kind of
differential between the mortgage and the worth of the house.

And then people talk about selling the land. That means
you'd have to get involved in the whole process of sweating
out the sale. Then you'd have to start hunting for another
place. And I'm not good at real estate. So all of these things
added up.

First we came to the decision that we were going to
rebuild if it were possible. But secondly, we didn't want to
smell of being defeated by this. We didn't want the kids to
come away with the feeling we had been defeated. It wasn't
just for the children; some of this was for ourselves too.

There is an overtone to all of this, you see—a kind of feeling that, I'll be damned if I let this thing do me in.

Thus, in the face of the overwhelming devastation of the storm, in the face of the initial impotence that it aroused, many people responded with an assertion of mastery and an unwillingness to bow before the fates. As the victim mobilized his energies, shook off his sense of daze, developed plans and hopes for the future, and explored the opportunities available to him, he often developed a heightened insistence upon his own self-determination and powers of recuperation.

The tasks of remobilization often were made easier by changes in the expectations of nonvictims. The social world of the city was changed by the tornado: for a time the usual rules and prescriptions for behavior were held in abeyance, and new ones, which better fitted the needs of the victims, were adopted. Here we simply note this as fact; the next chapter discusses this emergence of new norms in greater detail. While the emergency norms were in operation, they influenced most encounters between victims and nonvictims:

> We went out and had breakfast. The restaurant manager came up to the table and tried to find out whether we would like to put the meal on account. He tried to ask it in a way that wouldn't embarrass us. This was kind of an extension of the helpful behavior that people generally showed us.

The mood underlying such norms influenced all encounters, and not just those which involved the giving of help. Said a therapist of a case:

> She's a woman who is not really in much contact with her neighbors; she's a bit suspicious. But after the tornado she went out into the neighborhood, and she told me many conversations with neighbors across the street and even in the next block. This is more interaction with the neighbors

than I've ever heard her mention before. I think she was looking for some sort of mutual support.

While these emergency norms continued, they facilitated the rehabilitation process.

AFTEREFFECTS

Quick remobilization was not possible for everyone. Some victims were unable to form plans, others were unable to make use of opportunities. An example comes from a volunteer social worker who visited a victim one month after the tornado:

Miss Meedly is in need of help. She is a middle-aged Negro lady living alone. Right now her sister from California and the sister's baby are staying with her. Miss Meedly has difficulty of various kinds. She is an ex-TB patient and has one lung removed. She considers herself unemployable and probably is so. She fatigues easily. In addition, she seems to have limited intelligence and certainly has limited education.

Miss Meedly owns the house in which she lives. She is buying it through Barnet Real Estate Company. She has no idea whether Mr. Barnet took out any insurance on the house. Furthermore, she seems unable to mobilize herself sufficiently to look into the matter.

The house itself is in need of repairs; the roof is in very bad shape, the windows are broken; there is broken glass around; and the gas has been shut off because of a leak. Miss Meedly was told by the Red Cross to locate a plumber who would repair the gas main; she was also told to get some estimates on the roof repair and on the windows. But here, too, apparently she is unable to take any initiative. The printed words on the application are overwhelming to her. She has no idea of how to call the plumber or what to do. A further complication—she has no telephone in her house. So even to take the first step of making a telephone call, she has to walk either to a neighbor or to the corner. She seemed unable to do anything about this.

I feel that this woman is in need of help. She functions at a very low level of efficiency in general, and is entirely unable to cope with the emergencies and problems posed by the tornado. She is very eager for help and expressed her appreciation of my visit several times.

Here, then, was a failure of remobilization: plans were not made, apathy was not overcome, opportunities were neither comprehended nor taken. The fault lay both in the limited capabilities of the person and in the limited options which were realistically available to her. Such a response—or more accurately, lack of response—characterized a significant but proportionately small group of victims.

For most, however, the problems posed by the storm were dealt with effectively. Plans for remobilization solidified; the victims began to get on with their work. It was then that minor irritations assumed a more important role. For some, these irritations were held off for a while by a kind of role-playing: families tried to look upon the experience as a form of "camping out." An observer noted of an acquaintance:

His reaction and that of the younger boy seemed to be of people out on an overnight camping trip, roughing it, but not at all unhappy or really shocked by it. They were making the best of the situation.

However, as the days went by the strains of reconstruction mounted. People disliked showing their passes to get into the damaged area; squabbles developed with insurance adjusters; uncertainty about insurance coverage caused niggling dissatisfaction; and the extra burdens imposed by rebuilding claimed their toll. Life in a damaged home always had its problems:

There were moments of real discomfort. Tension builds up when four people are in the same bedroom. The basement in effect became one bedroom. The emergency character was over, and everybody was assuming more normal activities. So it came to feel as if it were just a bit of the drudgery.

This irritation with the constant accumulation of small problems and annoyances left a residue of irritability for some months after the storm.

For the majority of victims, though, life soon resumed its normal, expectable course. A therapist remarked with some surprise:

> It all blew over pretty fast. I wasn't hearing much about the tornado after two or three appointments. I think that's rather interesting. You'd think they'd talk about it for weeks, but they didn't.

To be a victim is an ephemeral thing; the reactions and the roles recede, and the changes become part of the ongoing continuity of life.

CHAPTER THREE

THE GROWTH OF EPHEMERAL ROLES: HELPERS, NEUTRALS, AND THE POST-DISASTER UTOPIA

OST PSYCHOLOGICAL STUDIES of disaster focus primarily upon the victims, but other people are as strongly affected. A community operates as a total system, and disruption of a single part can profoundly influence the whole. So it was with Topeka. The storm had repercussions not only for those caught in its path, but also for many others who went unscathed. This chapter is devoted to these others, and to the psychosocial impact of the storm among the nonvictims.

Of the nonvictims, we shall focus primarily upon those who took the "helping role"—those who volunteered their services in the interests of community rehabilitation. We shall consider the helping role itself: its motivations and its vicissitudes. As contrast, we shall also examine the role of the "neutral," the person to whom the tornado made no discernible behavioral difference.

Let us begin by looking at a single case.

A HELPER: MRS. BROWN

Mrs. Brown, a woman in her late twenties, lives on the prosperous west side of Topeka; her husband is employed by a local hospital. They have three children, and ordinarily her time is devoted to raising her children, an occasional extension class, and volunteer work for a local church. She and her husband are more conservative in outlook than the average Kansan; both had, for instance, worked for Barry Goldwater in the 1964 presidential campaign.

Their home lies five miles from the path of the tornado. When the sirens blew, they gathered in the basement and huddled around the portable radio. After the funnel passed, the father left for the hospital. At this point the children became upset, so that Mrs. Wilson had her hands full. She did, however, phone her church and offer overnight accommodation for any victims from the congregation.

On Thursday Mrs. Brown felt a strong need to do something more. Of course, she had to take care of the children, but she also had some time free. She wanted to help, but had no idea of what might be done. Her irresolution faded when she heard on the radio an appeal for used clothing. Mrs. Brown packed a box of old suits and dresses, put them in her car, and drove toward the clothing depot. Unfortunately, neither she nor the radio announcer had realized what this task entailed. The streets were jammed with traffic, and many of the usual routes were blocked by guards. The clothing remained undelivered.

This experience set her to thinking: if clothing was needed, some convenient collection points for it should be set up. She drove home and phoned the church secretary. The two of them agreed that the church could serve as a collection point. Once this was settled, Mrs. Brown phoned the radio station and asked for publicity.

By Friday morning she had established a clothing depot at the church, and secondhand blankets, suits, and dresses came pouring in. In the meantime, she had had another thought—what about the victims who needed some place to leave the children while they cleared away rubble? Here was a potential need, and she arranged for volunteers to run a nursery school at the church. As it turned out, there was not much demand for this—the victims seemed more interested in keeping their families together than in getting their children out of the way. Mrs. Brown put the nursery school volunteers to work sorting and packing clothing.

Indeed, Mrs. Brown had within two days developed and organized a small volunteer service. She gave direction not only to the volunteers, but to the church secretary and to one of the deacons. Mrs. Brown felt good about this; help was needed, and it was being supplied. Her ordinary roles—housewife and mother —were laid aside for the emergency; instead she was busily organizing and directing an essential service.

Almost immediately, however, two problems arose—problems which were to concern, in some way or another, most of the volunteer helpers. The first is exemplified by one man who may or may not have been a victim:

> He came in right away with his family and spent an hour selecting clothes. I felt a little suspicious about whether he really needed the clothes or not, because his car was not damaged in any way.
>
> The children told conflicting stories about whether the house was damaged. And I really began to get kind of angry, so I moved away from them. Someone else came and helped them. I said something to the minister, and he said, "Well,

they are in some kind of need; and I don't know whether its physical, moral, or spiritual."

I knew this was going to happen. Some people are going to go from agency to agency and collect as much as they could. And some people were really going to need the things. I decided that, under the circumstances, I had no valid reason for evaluating or judging.

In other words, for this helper a moral dilemma quickly arose: who deserved help? The norms were clear: victims needed help; freeloaders did not. But sometimes it was difficult to tell who was the bona fide victim, and who the freeloader. What had started as a crystal-clear standard came to have troubling complexities. After some initial soul-searching, Mrs. Brown decided simply to ignore the dilemma. During the emergency she adopted a nonjudgmental stance. She described her attitude as, "If you need it, take it." In her own way she had arrived at a new standard of value: from each according to his ability, to each according to his need.

The second conflict developed as Mrs. Brown came into contact with official agencies. Mrs. Brown developed strong feelings about the Red Cross workers:

They were very starched—you have to be careful with those starched uniforms. And they had white high heels.

I went down to the Central Red Cross Office, because some people wanted to send a message to their son in Viet Nam. In the central office I walked in, all dirty and unstarched—when I have to work I don't have a starched uniform, I wear jeans! I don't have an official tag and I didn't have a Red Cross patch. So I waited in line for fifteen minutes while some other people were taken care of. That was fine, I didn't mind that. But when it was my turn to get to the desk, the Red Cross people lit up cigarettes, sipped their coffee, and finally someone deigned to speak to me. I explained that I was bringing a message, and she said, "I'm sorry. We can't do anything about getting these messages to

Viet Nam." I became very angry, and I did something I have never done before. I started using names. I said I just came from talking with a lady who is a board member of the Red Cross, and I was told that the service could be had. Then I was quickly ushered through three offices to an air-conditioned one. In the office was a woman who was taking care of this message relay. Her first theme was that *no* messages could be gotten to Viet Nam.

Eventually the message was sent; the Red Cross member volunteered to write it and send it by air letter.

It would be a mistake to focus too much on particular incidents or particular frictions. Mrs. Brown's point was that the whole tone of the Red Cross was wrong. Somehow, she seemed to feel that different norms and different standards should be adopted during the emergency; she was incensed at the orderly business-as-usual air of the official organization:

> The Red Cross center was having interviews, and this seemed to be their goal—having interviews. Whatever happened to the people after the interview was none of their concern. If they had the papers left from the interview, the Red Cross was happy. The Red Cross workers became very cross about people coming into the relief center to get food for lunch; they were making too much noise! The workers said they couldn't hear the interview, and so a friend of mine suggested that they might sit on the same side of the desk with the person they were interviewing. Well, the Red Cross people were astonished; their mouths dropped open six feet.

Such official demands and expectations were seen by Mrs. Brown as lacking in human compassion:

> There was a couple who came to the distribution center. They were getting the things that they needed, and were ready to leave for the car. Just at that point a Starched Uniform ran after them and said, "Oh, I'm sorry! You will have to bring all those things back! They haven't been checked

out to you!" This robbing the people of personal dignity just kills me. So they came back, and they remained very submissive, and they went through it all.

Implicit in these examples are two notions: that emergency victims should not be expected to conform to rules, regulations, and paperwork; and that such bureaucratic privileges as coffee breaks while clients waited were inappropriate in the disaster situation. Ordinarily, such petty annoyances would have been casually accepted. Other deviations from usual behavior also are apparent; usually, Mrs. Brown would not go downtown wearing dirty jeans, but in this situation they served her almost as a uniform of office.

Mrs. Brown continued with volunteer work throughout the next week, punctuated only by one day devoted to household activities: "They made me take the day off; I think it was a conspiracy between my husband and the minister at the church." But during the next week her activities changed markedly:

The whole thrust changed in the clothing situation. We weren't running a floating rummage sale anymore.

The new thing was, could we do laundry? People had clothes that were dirty from the storm, and they didn't have water. They didn't have power, and they didn't have transportation to go to laundromats. So he went over to East Topeka and colected truckloads of laundry in separate packs. We brought them over here to the laundromats and got them clean.

This again was an unusual reversal of roles: a middle-class white woman taking in washing from a predominantly Negro clientele.

Besides these activities, Mrs. Brown became personally involved with two Negro women, both welfare clients with small children. She set herself the task of finding housing for them. This turned out to be difficult; two days were needed to work through its complications. In the course of this adventure she sometimes became disturbed at the attitudes of other helpers:

Another thing happened which made me angry. A gentleman looked at me over their heads and said, "Oh, you are doing your good deed for the day," and winked. As if I was Mrs. Bountiful-Do-Good! I became incensed. I said, "I'm not doing my damn good deed for the day," and I wanted him to know it too. I don't care how inconceivable it is to him—I can ride in a car with a person of any skin color. And its none of his blankety-blank business whether I do or not.

One cannot help but feel that Mrs. Brown's embattled vehemence came from the unusual role in which she found herself: helping a pregnant Negro lady cut through the red tape of welfare bureaucracy was not something she was likely to do every day of the week.

But the helping role was temporary. It lasted for ten days after the tornado and then faded away. Quite simply, the immediate tasks were done, and for the long-range effort specialized agencies moved in. Like many helpers, Mrs. Brown soon went back to her usual routines. For some time afterward she felt a sense of kinship with others who had worked on volunteer projects. Occasionally this kinship had a slight competitive overtone: people would ironically comment on the phenomenon of "volunteermanship"—the "I-put-in-more-hours-than-anyone" gambit. In time this too faded, and the experience was stored away as a memory, to be brought out and unfolded on special occasions.

ON TAKING THE HELPER ROLE

The adventures of Mrs. Brown were shared in some degree by many Topekans who volunteered their services after the storm. It was a dramatic and exciting time, a time when the impossible seemed likely and the improbable became an everyday occurrence. The emergence of a helping role was transient, but socially important and personally significant. Its growth, development, and decay deserves examination as a thing in itself.

The tornado had immediate and strong psychological re-percussions for many Topekans outside the path. They felt a pressing sense of tension—a desire to do something, anything. This tension was reported in many ways: "angry" . . . "restless after the tornado" . . . "had the fidgets" . . . "everybody there was all shook up." This anxiety was usually coupled with an urge to help, to attack the disaster and aid its victims. From other disasters come accounts of similar reactions. Moore (1958, p. 313) reporting on the Waco and San Angelo tornado, says of the "rescue period": "Intense activity quickly follows—an effort to effective reorganization by the use of physical strength and vigor. . . . The situation still is not seen clearly and rationally, but action is demanded as a means of reasserting control. . . ."

Similar observations are made by Wallace 1956, pp. 141, 142–43) in the Worcester tornado; he contrasts the dazed re-action of the "disaster syndrome" with its counterpart, "the counter-disaster syndrome":

. . . the essential characteristic in the counter-disaster syndrome is over-consciousness and hyperactivity . . . the first stage which prevails chiefly during the period of rescue, evacuation, and emergency medical care is characterized by extreme anxiety, with a profusion of autonomic symptoms: tachycardia, shortness of breath, sweating, muscular cramps, etc. The rescue worker is likely to overexert himself physically, sometimes to the point of collapse . . . the sufferer is likely to prefer working on his own or to take a position of responsibility. He does a great deal of work, and its value is considerable but it is apt to be hastily done and it may require checking and possibly redoing by less emotionally involved personnel.

This state has been described further by Moore (1958, p. 313), who speaks of a post-disaster "demand for activity," and by William Menninger (1952), who describes a desire among volunteers to do something—almost anything—that would be helpful.

As we have noted, this urge for action led to an immediate mass convergence on the disaster area. Others, who heeded the radio and television requests to stay home, felt indecisive and frustrated. One woman describes the initial dilemma:

My most immediate reaction was worrying about my friends. The street that seemed to be the worst was right around where they lived. I would have stopped and gone into the area, but they were making the cars go on through. And I didn't know if there was anything I could do to help. Through all that day, which seemed like one of the longest days of my life, I sat around waiting for news at the office; waiting and wondering if there was anything I could do.

Nor were the people who swarmed to the scene necessarily less frustrated:

I drove along the street and stopped several times and offered to help people. Houses were gone and everything was just cleaned off. There weren't many people coming out of the houses. And I thought, "My God, there must be people dead in these houses!" I went to see if I could help anybody, but everyone seemed to be okay. There wasn't much I could do, so I just went to check on my business for a few minutes; then I went back home and didn't do much after that.

For many who felt a strong push to help, the initial state of indecision led to a strong feeling of uselessness. A would-be helper said, "With no tools and organization, no structure within which to work, I was completely immobilized."

Such initial frustration was not true of everyone. Many people felt no desire to help; others felt the desire to help and had the means at hand. It depended upon one's place in the social fabric. Some saw an immediate need for services they could offer; this was especially true of physicians, hospital employees, auxiliary policemen, and the like. Others had resources which could be quickly brought to bear, and which could serve an emergency need. Usually these people took the initiative. An observer reported:

The principal at Jardine Junior High School thought to himself, "My school is close, and if there is that much destruction we are going to need shelter." And he was absolutely right. This is what all the principals thought, at least in that part of town. At McEachron School the principal was there right away, and at Maude Bishop the principal was there very soon after the tornado went through.

In general, those who had access to a potential helping service or organization were quick to volunteer its use. Similarly, those whose relatives or friends had suffered damage immediately focused upon the immediate need. Kinship ties provided a structure and a means for helping.

For others who were in positions of responsibility directly related to disaster, other dilemmas arose. They were responsible; they had an ascribed role for dealing with disaster. But sometimes they had trouble deciding exactly what to do:

We started down the street, and it finally came upon me that I was an official of the Shawnee County Chapter of the Red Cross. So I told my wife I had better go to the Chapter House. When I got there Ben gave me a yellow pad of paper, and told me to do what he had always done in our disaster practices—go out and survey the area. So I did. But when I got out there I was overwhelmed. I said, "This is ridiculous!" What we had done before was to practice on a block or two, where you could go in and check it down. But this looked to me like the town was wiped out. I didn't know what to do.

I walked through the area and somebody said, "Red Cross is up at the School." So I walked toward it; all I was doing then was trying to get out and help in that school as a volunteer. The captain of the guard ran up to me. I certainly was frightened for a minute as he addressed me as somebody who knew what to do under these circumstances. Up there everybody was trying to find anything they could do to help. They were looking out in that area and not knowing what to do. Finally there was a fellow—and I don't know his name—he was one of these take-charge men, and he pretty well took charge and started directing us around. He got the thing into methodical order. The rest of us immediately fell in just doing anything this man wanted. In fact, I was looking for somebody to tell me what to do.

As this example shows clearly, the official disaster roles were occasionally inappropriate, and new roles and positions developed in their place.

The need for temporary leadership, as exemplified by the "take-charge man" in the example cited above, and by Mrs. Brown, led many to assume tasks for which they had no special competence. Somebody had to do the job and people volunteered. Since most of the helpers were looking for direction and for social organization, such leadership was seldom challenged. One such leader told how it came about:

And then I said I'd do the search. I had no idea of what I was talking about. I just said I would do it. By this time a guy from Civil Defense in Missouri had already arrived at the scene. He said he had done "search" before and knew what needed to be done. So he aligned himself with us in the search parties.

We went to the Police Station and I was asked what I was going to do. How was I going to organize the search party and how many men did I need, how many vehicles, and that sort of thing? I just started bluffing and kept right on. I gave answers and told them what we were going to do, just as if I had done it before. Everyone fell in line, so that I had the best of cooperation at that point. I have done more conning in the last week than I had done in ten years.

From these "seed crystals" of social organization, a ramifying network of services developed. Areas in which volunteer energies were needed became increasingly apparent. Subsidiary tasks were defined, volunteers were enlisted in social units to meet the task needs, and out of the combination of task and group grew more specific roles.

During this period, life changed for most helpers; their old and usual roles were held in suspension. This transient phase may be labeled a time of "role moratorium." In place of old roles they took on new and ephemeral roles, which sometimes led to arresting changes in social perception. We have seen how, for Mrs. Brown, the new role tasks forced a temporary shift in attitudes and behavior. A Negro minister commented on his experience in working at an emergency center:

> Whenever disaster strikes everybody becomes as one—they function as a unit. There is no such thing as high and low. Those who were poverty-stricken worked right along with those who were real rich; there were no cross words. They just picked up their utensils and went to work. Once a rich lady went to the kitchen and started to do dishes like it was second nature—she forgot about class and catered to the people who were in need.

With the role moratorium, people laid aside many other distinguishing attributes. Some, in fact, felt a sense of anonymity. Reflected a volunteer,

> I realized that I never even learned the names of any members of my crew. Another man and I had some similar army experiences, and we shared them with each other, but impersonally. We spoke of events and situations, but not of ourselves. In a sense, this anonymity seems appropriate. I'm not sure in what way, but it seems as though the scope of the storm is so great that individual names, or individualities themselves, are meaningless in the face of the damage and destruction. All during the time I was directing the efforts of our group I was not conscious of myself as an individual at all, only as a factor in the so-far unorganized effort to do something.

With the suspension of usual roles came a certain suspension of the individual identity itself.

This is not to say that all helpers engaged in a total role moratorium, or became part of an impersonal and faceless mass. Two weeks after the tornado, a volunteer social worker commented on the role limitations she and others brought to the task:

> I think everyone rallied to the occasion, and wanted to do what needed to be done. But at the same time the helpers were confined, in a sense, because of their own way of functioning. Although there was quite a bit of sympathy and empathy, it was hard to get out from the usual role one played in daily life.
>
> A lot of people came wanting to help, but with certain specific things in mind. But if we're going to look at a human situation and meet human needs, you can't say (for example) that you are going to do social work. I was most irritated at some of the social workers with whom I had contact. Because you can still do social work—you can still use what you have as a social worker—by working in the clothing area and picking up things. I asked one woman to check on a family which might be in need, and she said, "Maybe you can send somebody out just to check up; I'd rather do something else." In an emergency operation one has to be prepared to pick up and move in. But for them it seemed almost like an office situation. And some of the professionals stood around and did nothing when nobody came in. But there were things to be done right there at the center—you could just sweep the floor if it was needed. But this some of them couldn't do.

So the role moratorium was relative, and even in the beginning many people tended to choose ephemeral roles for which they had some skill, and to avoid others which they felt to be incongruent with their status.

HELPING AS A ROLE

The moratorium on day-to-day roles was strongly motivated. At first the nature of the new role was unclear; it emerged from the circumstances and led to new forms of social organization. As such new forms of social organization became available, the nature of the ephemeral role became more clear. Group norms and values developed. Here we shall discuss the emergent characteristics of this ephemeral role, and the relationship of such characteristics to the general social and individual tasks confronting the helper.

Normally, a role is defined as the expectable behavior which accompanies any given social position. Much role behavior is directly relevant to the function of the position: the salesman sells, the psychiatrist gives psychotherapy, and the cobbler cobbles. These role tasks and their means of fulfillment are prescribed by social expectations. Usually people enter a role which is already available; it is as if the role were a house that came complete with furniture and decorations. Role behavior may also develop in response to conflicts within the role, as a means of warding off unpleasant situations. Generally, people move toward roles which fit easily with their pre-existing roles or with their idealized self; there thus comes to be an increasingly close fit between role and personality.

The helper's role, ephemeral and emergent, was rather different. Helpers found no prefabricated social position, no prescribed sets of behaviors into which they moved. Rather, the role expectations developed as the emergent social systems appeared. Thus, in talking about the ephemeral "helping role," we are talking about an evolutionary development, and about a role which was different in kind from most within the social world. The role itself developed to meet the tasks imposed by tornado reconstruction.[3]

What were the characteristics and vicissitudes of this new and temporary role? The case of Mrs. Brown shows some of the features encountered among most volunteer helpers. First, the role allowed and encouraged heightened activity and aggression. Some volunteers spoke of "fighting with destruction," and this militancy was not unusual. Several heart attacks occurred when sedentary office workers put in eight to ten hours a day chopping

---

[3] The concept of "ephemeral role" is developed in greater detail by Zurcher (1968, pp. 283–84).

limbs and clearing away debris; such ferocity was beyond their physical tolerance. Many helpers saw the storm as an enemy needing to be attacked.

Second, the role provided a set of moral absolutes. Storm destruction was Bad; helping victims was Good. As a concomitant, aggression was justified against any barrier which stood in the way. The role allowed aggression to be displayed against physical objects, and against uncooperative agency people, in a way which would not normally occur.

Third, the role existed to provide helpful encounters between victim and helper. Anything that stood in the way of helping was seen as inappropriate. This meant that the helpers expected many normal procedures to be laid aside during the emergency. Rules and regulations got in the way of the personalistic helping relationship. Bureaucracy was intolerable. The role moratorium was extended to the social scene. Usual social procedures were to be held in suspension. The helpers expected a moratorium not only on bureaucratic procedures, but also on social distinctions. For the time being, all men were brothers and the barriers of social position were swept aside. The result was a remarkable spirit of community cohesion.

HELPING AND THE REWARDS OF THE POST-DISASTER UTOPIA

Here again the experience of Topeka seems typical. This period of disaster response has even been dignified with a name, "the post-disaster Utopia" (Wolfenstein, 1957, pp. 189, 191). Her description could have been written of Topeka:

> Following a disaster there is apt to be great upsurge of goodwill and helpfulness among the survivors and on the part of outsiders who come to their aid. . . . In normal times people are suspicious of strangers who approach them; the presumption is that their motives are not benevolent. Strangers who approach each other in a disaster-stricken time are more readily assumed to be helpful and generous in their

intentions. Where in ordinary times compassion for the unfortunate is often qualified by doubts whether it is not their own fault, in a disaster the worthiness of the victims is beyond question. So, for example, in England many who had suffered alone, without sympathy, during the depression, discovered the joys of generous support and friendly assistance during the war time bombings.

The ephemeral helping role was carried out as a highly separate set of behaviors, largely unintegrated with other roles. As noted above, this was not an absolute matter, but the tendency was distinctly there. A helper expressed it thus:

> It was kind of two worlds that existed. I was going at certain hours, and coming home to my nice home after that. It was unreal in a sense, and it hit me. I had to see how I fitted into these two worlds, and I had to think in terms of myself shifting from one to the other. Sometimes it made me uncomfortable.

The helping role was a thing apart from the rest of life.

As time went on, the role became more specific, more defined and articulated. Helpers tended to focus upon specific tasks. Some things they defined as within their scope, other things were outside. Role *specialization* grew as the social structures developed and became more distinct. Helpers came to symbolize their role, usually by their dress. Office workers removed their ties even though they might be sitting behind desks, thus signaling their willingness to throw themselves into the helping transaction. Other middle-class people appeared in ancient jeans and paint-stained T-shirts; occasionally such garb seemed to serve as a uniform. All these visible signs emphasized their identity with the role.

Helping had its own rewards. Sometimes the rewards were provided by the victims themselves, in the coin of gratitude. When helpers talked of their experiences, they would focus on certain defining incidents—incidents wherein gratitude was expressed:

> This one lady we ran into lived next to the Interstate highway—she was an old lady, and after we got through cleaning up, we cleaned up part of her yard. She just broke down and cried she was so thankful.

Often such defining encounters would be contrasted with others in which no reward was forthcoming. In such cases the helpers seemed to feel shortchanged:

> The next place we went to, this fellow was cutting up trees with his son. We walked over and asked if we could help him. And he said, "Yeah." So we got our chainsaws and started sawing away—there were about nine of us guys working. And as soon as we got started, the son says, "Say, looks like we got somebody to do our work for us. Why don't we sit down and watch them." You know, on the first day out that's kind of discouraging. The guy didn't appreciate it—he didn't give a darn.

At times the reward of gratitude was forthcoming, but not always.

Other workers noted a different kind of reward, a kind of group closeness, a sharing, which came with the helping role:

> In response to our requests as to what we might do to help, she paused and then—amazingly enough—said that she wanted to have her windows washed and the kitchen cleaned up. My husband and son proceeded to wash all of her windows both inside and out and I scrubbed her kitchen cupboards and mopped her kitchen floor. For the first hour or so she was relatively uncommunicative and simply sat slouched in the chair. Although I had introduced myself at our first meeting, she did not tell me her name or anything about herself for some time. Gradually it became apparent that she was having difficulty moving about and breathed very heavily. She broke the silence by poignantly asking me, "Why are you so nice to me? Who are you? Where do

you live?" She asked these questions during the afternoon, as though she found it impossible to believe that I, who lived in a nice undamaged home, would be willing to scrub her house.

Somehow convinced that I really wanted to help, she began to tell me about herself. She was a widow in relatively poor health. She managed to keep her home by staying during the day with an older invalid who demanded little care but needed someone with her. Mrs. H. herself was suffering from arthritis and high blood pressure which had been tremendously aggravated by her tornado experience.

One informant captured this kind of reward in a single sentence, saying, "I was caught up in a certain pleasure and satisfaction in meeting all the new people in East Topeka, being impressed by their fortitude and poise."

Still another reward came from the developing *esprit de corps* of the work group. The warfare against a common enemy provided satisfactions for many. Said one young Mennonite worker:

> Well, I told my pastor that I have never been proud to be a Mennonite but I'm proud to be a Mennonite now. And I said, the response just brings tears to your eyes, to think that so many people would come out. It really made me feel good, that so many people would come four hundred or five hundred miles to help. One man got up at 2:30 A.M. to be sure he got here on time. Sure it would be a lot easier to be a Presbyterian or a Baptist or something; then you wouldn't have to worry about all these people asking questions—if your dad wears a beard and all this kind of stuff, and what kind of square are you? But you do something like this and it makes you feel kind of good.

Such rewards were social and generally shared; they resulted from the transaction between helpers and victims, and were noted by most of the relief workers.

More idiosyncratic motivations also were apparent. For

some of the helpers, the exciting work of rescue gave proof of competence. One therapist discussed a patient in such terms:

I have another case, a very action-oriented young man who works for a local institution. He was very much in the forefront of the rescue and clean-up operations. As soon as the tornado hit he was out there directing traffic, helping to get people out of the hardest hit areas. The next day he got a volunteer crew out there helping. He worked very hard, very effectively. The tornado provided a chance for him to demonstrate prowess, control, assertiveness, and masculinity in the face of some overwhelming natural force. This young man has a great deal of conflict around masculinity. His self-image is that of a puny, weak, helpless homosexual. This is an image against which he struggles, and the tornado provided him with a matchless outlet for a role which denies the unconscious self-concept. I must say, however, that from everything I heard his behavior was adaptive and helpful, despite its "fitting in" with his underlying difficulties. It was quite appropriate.

Similar dynamics, although described in different terms, were implied by another therapist's description:

This patient is about eighteen, and in general he's not particularly motivated to participate in social activities except for his own pleasure. He was asked if he would participate as a volunteer. As time went by he began to feel some satisfaction from the work, being part of it and being helpful. He would talk about it with some enthusiasm, somehow feeling a part of things and feeling more important. He felt he was doing something that was needed—which to him was a new experience. Part of his difficulty is that he always felt that he wasn't needed. He has felt that it would be hard for him to do anything to measure up to what his family has achieved, or what they might expect of him. But the work gave him a good feeling about himself and his ability to contribute—he felt worth while, you know.

Here again, the helper role demonstrated—to the helper as well as to others—a potential for competence and mastery.

Occasionally people were rewarded by a reduction of guilt:

Another patient responded with the sense of guilt and the vague feeling of being overprivileged because so many people had suffered such loss. Fortune had somehow spared her, and there was great guilt over this. The guilt was clearly expressed. She felt selfish in coming to psychotherapy. This woman has a great deal of conflict over her role as a housewife and as a woman; she feels a great deal of guilt over many things, and the tornado provided her with another outlet to express that guilt. So she felt that she deserved punishment, and was guilty that the tornado missed such a "bad" person as herself.

Thus guilt could provide motivation for action.

Such motives, coupled with the emergency norms and the moratorium on usual roles, sometimes led to marked behavioral changes. For a time the usual problems and strains of life were laid aside. Neurotic symptoms abated:

It cured her depression in a kind of way. After the tornado hit she was down at the Red Cross within a few hours, and spent the next thirty days as a volunteer. She canceled all her appointments with me. She was driving a Red Cross truck sixteen hours a day, cooking, baking, chauffeuring, delivering, and getting other volunteers. She put in a tremendous amount of energy and effort in getting people to work.

She got involved in all these activities, and it helped. One of her difficulties was a complete lack of things to do. She seemed to find herself through the tornado. She has become reinvolved and interested in things that she had given up a year or two ago when the depression started.

There is something else: this woman has a great deal of difficulty in expressing her angry feelings. But she ran into a friend who did something she was very strongly opposed to, and so she was able to express hostility. And then her husband took off on a fishing trip on June 10. She has been openly critical of him ever since he ran out. She might have been intolerant before, but she isn't guilty about it this time.

This case was not unique; two other therapists reported similar remobilization in their depressed patients.

Such behavioral change appears to result from the close fit between the "helper role" and the dynamics of depression. The depressed person often has strong feelings of anger and disappointment, which are blocked from expression by excessive guilt. In depression the anger is turned inward against the self, so the individual feels incompetent and worthless. Especially is this so when the life circumstances give few opportunities for meaningful affection, or for the development of basic self-esteem. The role of the helper provided an escape from such dilemmas. The role tasks were clear-cut, and obviously meaningful. To be a helper was to be on the side of the angels; aggression was permissible since the ends were so clear and so valued. Residual anxieties could be dissipated in motoric expression. Finally, the sheer grubbiness of much of the work—its low status implications—carried two meanings: it was Good because it involved self-sacrifice, and it also met characterological needs for punishment. It would be hard to imagine a social role more congruent with the dynamics of certain types of depression.

These then were the components—the motivations and the rewards—which in our interviews seemed to underlie the "postdisaster Utopia." But in the nature of things, utopia is transient:

. . . it tends to break down as time goes on. Partly, negative feelings toward people recuperate. The love that was felt in a situation of life and death becomes mitigated by reviving annoyances and antagonisms as things return to normal. Those who have volunteered to help their enthusiasm waning, their tasks becoming a chore, as the atmosphere of an extreme situation becomes dissipated. . . . Usual attitudes about giving and taking are re-established. Habits of independence and self-sufficiency complicate the acceptance of further aid. Suspicions arise about people who readily accept the help of relief agencies [Wolfenstein, 1957, p. 193].

In Topeka, too, class and status distinctions which had been laid aside were soon picked up again. In the place of the humane transactions of utopia, the regular bureaucratic and business procedures emerged once more.

NONHELPERS: THE NEUTRAL STANCE

So far we have focused upon the helper who participated in organized volunteer activities. To be sure, even among the organized volunteers, a spectrum of helping efforts existed: some put in only a few hours, while others worked full-time for several weeks. Many more people served outside of volunteer organizations, helping friends or relatives sort through the rubble, assisting in finding new homes, and providing shelter and comfort. Such help was of great importance. But this is only one end of the spectrum.

There is a qualitative difference between even the most casual of helpers and those who did nothing. The other end of the spectrum too deserves examination.

It was noted earlier that the helping role developed among people who were motivated to take part in the recovery tasks, and who had some social structure available for such participation. For those who gave help outside of volunteer organizations, the kinship and friendship ties provided a kind of social structure and social motivation. But what led to the neutral stance? Was it lack of motivation? If so, what were the roots of this lack? Or was it perhaps that social structures provided little opportunity for participation? These are the issues we shall now discuss.

Before beginning, however, one proviso should be noted: our material on nonhelpers comes largely from interviews with psychotherapists. The cases are therefore biased in the direction of psychopathology; we can see certain patterns, but the prevalence of such patterns is unknown. Nonetheless, the patterns themselves make sense in the total context of the community.

For a person to be motivated toward the helper role, there must be some sense of shared identification, empathy, or concern for others. Much of our material indicates that nonhelpers were deficient in such empathy. This lack was seen sometimes among people who functioned well:

I have one patient who is a professional man. His profession was in demand after the tornado, and so was his wife's profession. Neither of them have made a gesture toward offering their skills. It made me angry. These people are isolated from the Topeka community to a great extent. But they are not isolated people, they have friends. But they have no roots or connections with the Topeka community. I think the basic problem is a problem of empathy. I mean, I think both of them are internally focused, people who are more interested in themselves than anything else. Their relationships with others have a kind of shallow quality.

The lack of empathy was most pronounced among the psychiatrically ill:

Well, this one man is a very disabled fellow, chronically so for years, and I'm always amazed when he can extend himself to anyone. His inability to get involved with life is such a problem with him that I'd have fallen out of the chair if he said he had volunteered his services. With him it's just a general kind of uninvolvement with others.

Or again:

One other patient is just an awfully young fellow. He isn't mature enough to know that people help others. I used his noninvolvement as a means of showing that this is a way of avoiding life. What is it with him that he couldn't get a little more involved? But that's so common in all of his reactions that I hardly need a tornado to prove my point.

Such lack of empathy, based upon narcissistic preoccupation, characterized seven of the fourteen nonhelpers reported by the psychotherapists.

As for the others, a slight lack of empathy was sometimes

strongly reinforced by lack of reference group indentification with the particular community:

> I have another patient who wasn't involved. He never thought of being involved. There are many things that he could have done; he is skilled in manual work. But it never occurred to him. His family is in another community, and he goes back there three or four times a week, even though he has a house up here in Topeka and his job is here. He doesn't feel like a Topekan. I feel sure that if the storm had hit the place where his family was he would have been active.
>
> And another deeper factor is, he is a fairly suspicious sort of man. It is hard for him to involve himself and to mix into other people's affairs.

Sometimes too the nonhelpers were so preoccupied with their own realistic struggles that help was out of the question:

> This is a very busy man who has just begun to be successful in his life, and he really works a good sixteen hours a day. He's the kind of man who actually has a great deal of feeling for others; he's a very affable, warm person, but as I say, he's so darn busy . . . and his survival currently demands that he be busy. He really cannot drop one step; if he does, everything gets behind. I think with him it's just a matter of having to keep up with his job.

Two other cases were similarly unable to act because of their own reality limitations: both were people who were struggling with difficult and debilitating physical illness.

In some cases the initial desire to help was not present; in other cases real barriers stood in the way. However, we ourselves interviewed no one who was unable to find effective ways of helping.

In sum, by looking at the motivation of nonhelpers, we can understand better the motivations underlying the helping role. If one was to become a helper, a pre-existing sense of identification with the stricken group or with the city was necessary.

People differed greatly in their sense of indentification; some had an identification with the whole collectivity of the city, while others restricted their identification to family and friends. For some, the identity extended no farther than their own skins.

One form of this sense of shared fate, of involvement with others, is sometimes spoken of as "reference group identity," but here we are pointing to a more general phenomenon. Before the tornado few of the volunteers would have thought of the total city and its populace as a major reference group. In the ordinary course of events, few, for example, would have considered their fate to be intertwined with that of the city's low-income Negro. Yet in a time of crisis a latent identification emerged, not with specific and delimited groups, but with the totality of the city in which Negroes, like others, were included. This capacity for extension of identity would seem the most crucial precursor of helping behavior.

We may thus view the "counter-disaster syndrome"—the agitation, hyperactivity, and frantic push toward recovery—as a logical outcome of the newly mobilized sense of shared community identity which was always latent for many, but not all, Topekans. By attacking the city the tornado was felt to have attacked the individual as well. The resultant mobilization and counter-attack was only to be expected. For those who felt part of their identity to be threatened, all trivial tasks, all customary roles and stations, were laid aside while the emergency was met. From this collective dynamic grew the "post-disaster Utopia" with its rich efflorescence of social activities and forms: a social phenomenon which for the period of crisis transfigured the city.

CHAPTER FOUR

THE EPHEMERAL GROUP

OCUSING UPON the individual tells much about the motivations underlying social action, but little about the forms of social behavior which emerged from such motivations. Although individual feelings and needs influenced the way groups behaved, the group process had its own dynamics and its own characteristics. In this chapter we shall describe the way in which the agitation, empathy, hyperactivity, and aggression of the "counter-disaster syndrome" led volunteer helpers to coalesce into small groups, and how the disaster setting, the individual motives, and structure provided by work tasks quickly led to rather special group processes. We shall spell out, in some detail, the ways in which a single work crew came together, melded into a unit, and then dissolved. In so doing, we shall examine, in microcosm, the specifically *social* dynamics which, writ large, influenced the tone and organization of the entire city.

Twenty-four hours after the tornado had passed, an emergency relief center for volunteer activities was set up in the low-income area of East Topeka. Inside the center, victims could find clothing, food, shelter, legal counsel, medical aid, and Red Cross registration; outside, groups of volunteers formed work crews and went into the neighborhood, removing tree limbs, clearing debris, bringing aid to homebound families, and fitting plastic sheets over damaged roofs and broken windows. The institutional development of the Volunteer Center will be described in Chapter 5; here it is enough to note that it provided a nuclear structure for the formation of small work groups made up of volunteers.

The very existence of a centralized and coordinating agency for volunteer activity produced a degree of role specialization among the would-be helpers. Some volunteers reported to the center in groups and knew each other well; others came alone and as strangers. Some chose desk work, counseling, or kitchen activities; others took on heavy manual labor. This chapter describes one particular type of work group: its members chose manual labor; most of them came as strangers to each other; all were personally untouched by the tornado; and none had relatives or friends needing assistance. Though exact figures are not available, it is estimated that during the course of the recovery effort twenty-five similar work groups existed, averaging about eight men per crew. These groups began their work on Friday morning, June 10, almost thirty-six hours after the storm. They coalesced during the period that has variously been called the "rehabilitation" (Wallace, 1956, p. 125), "emergency" (Form and Nosow, 1958, p. 17), "remedy" (Powell, Finesinger, and Greenhill, 1954, p. 5), or "recoil" (Glass, 1959, p. 222) stage of community response to disaster. Thus, the work crew described here represents a relatively late-blooming volunteer activity, with a group dynamic different from the more individual and unorganized rescue behavior occurring during the first few hours after impact. The group dynamics of the volunteer work crew were also different from those found within a formal organization, and from those found in more normal circumstances. This crew typified that transitional period during which, through emergency social systems, fractured components of the community were reknit and the individual needs of the helping participants were assuaged.

THE WORK CREW FORMS

By Friday morning thirty-six hours after the tornado, volunteers were gathering at the Volunteer Center, then entering the disaster-stricken area. Among these volunteers was a heavy-equipment operator, a civil defense employee, an undergraduate student, and one of the authors of this book, Dr. Louis Zurcher. These four volunteers formed the initial nucleus of a volunteer work crew, which worked at removing fallen trees and limbs from damaged or endangered houses. This small group stayed together for three days. During the first day it grew to six mem-

TABLE 1

"CORE" VOLUNTEER WORK CREW MEMBERS

Ephemeral Role	Days Worked*	"Civilian" Occupation	Age
Contactman	1,2,3	Social psychologist	30
Climber I	1,3	Heavy equipment operator	48
Sawman I	1,2,3	Civil defense employee	31
Climber II	1,2,3	Undergraduate student	20
Monsterman	1,2,3	House painter	40+
Roper I	1,2	Extension worker	38
Rigger	2,3	Writer	25
Roper II	2,3	Clinical psychologist	43
Sawman II	2,3	Commodities inspector	50+
Monster Assistant	2,3	House painter	40+

* 1 = Friday; 2 = Sunday; 3 = Sunday.

bers; by mid-Saturday it had fourteen; and on Sunday it had
nine (see Table 1). Volunteers came and went, but the group
was given stability by the presence of ten "core" members—
people who stayed with the work crew at least two days out of

TABLE 2

STATEMENTS INDICATING HOW "CORE" MEMBERS DISCOVERED
THE VOLUNTEER WORK CREW, AND THEIR MOTIVATIONS
FOR VOLUNTEERING

Ephemeral Role	*Statements*
Contactman	". . . felt restless after the tornado . . . angry . . . helpless . . . wanted to do something . . . heard from friend about plans to start an Emergency Relief Center . . . went down right away to see what I could do . . . assigned to sector maps for work parties, but there were no work parties . . . got impatient . . . decided to start one. . . ."
Climber I	". . . had the fidgets, so left my house and just wandered around . . . someone told me about the center, so I drifted over that way . . . saw Contactman with some tools, and I wanted to dig in, so I joined him. . . ."
Sawman I	". . . I'd been working for Civil Defense only a week before the tornado . . . worked pulling people out of wreckage, gave first aid . . . people kept looking to me to tell them what to do. . . . I did okay but God I was scared—only a week! . . . the next day assigned to drive around in my truck and take a survey . . . felt like I was wasting my time . . . felt like I should have been on the outside of the truck doing the work . . . then I was told to stop and do what I could . . . got my chain saw . . . went over to East Topeka and saw these guys hacking away at this tree on top of a car . . . asked them if they could use a man with a power saw, they hollered "Yes!" so I joined them."
Climber II	". . . was staying with a friend who lived near the Center . . . wanted to get with it, so I went over and asked what I could do . . . someone pointed to some guys down the street who were chopping away . . . went there and started chopping too. . . ."

TABLE 2 (*Continued*)

Ephemeral Role	Statements
Monsterman	". . . am a Civil Defense volunteer . . . had one of their trucks with a winch . . . told to look around . . . went to Emergency Relief Center. . . . Contactman was there getting some more tools . . . took me out to the crew . . . was glad to get out where there was some action."
Roper I	". . . I knew a lot of the people in East Topeka, because I have lived there, and because my job took me there. . . . I heard about the Emergency Center from some of the people who were working there . . . went to the center, then joined the work gang because I wanted to attack the damned mess directly, and not in some office. . . ."
Rigger	". . . was back at my job . . . felt out of place talking about the tornado . . . not yet time for talk . . . felt ineffectual . . . mounting sense of frustration . . . wanted to do something meaningful, now, as a release for some of the feelings that had been building up inside . . . not doing anything worth while . . . try to find some way or place to be useful . . . that night watch TV and learn that the Emergency Relief Center is calling for volunteers. . . respond instinctively . . . here is a place where I might be effective after all . . . at center I was told about Contactman's crew and where it was . . . found them, and went to work. . . ."
Roper II	". . . felt, I guess, vaguely overprivileged, vaguely guilty about having a house that was untouched in the face of so much damage . . . sense of frustration . . . feeling I wanted to do something . . . got a phone call from a friend at the Emergency Relief Center, asking for help . . . wanted to become directly involved in a counter-attack upon the disaster . . . went to the center Saturday morning, and a fellow said, 'there's Contactman and he's looking for some guys to work on a crew.' I said 'Fine' . . . and that's when I joined. . . ."
Monster Assistant	". . . I heard from some of the other Civil Defense volunteers about the Emergency Center . . . sounded like I could get into the swim there . . . found Monsterman and rode out to the crew with him. . . ."

the three. In this chapter, each core member is identified not by name, but by a title describing his major duty with the work crew. These men, with variable backgrounds and skills, were thrown together solely because they had volunteered. Except for Roper II and Rigger, none had previously been acquainted.

What led them to volunteer for this particular job? Asked this question after the crew disbanded, their answers were varied; but most emphasized the need to do something, to be active, to counter a sense of frustration and impotence. Some expressed a particular identification with, or concern for, the problems of the low-income area (see Table 2).

These volunteers were no different from the other helpers discussed in Chapter 3; they too felt the agitation and the expanded identity pressures of the counter-disaster syndrome. The result for *each* member was the urge to "dig in"—as the dynamics of the first day clearly reflect.

THE FIRST DAY OF THE WORK CREW

By Friday mid-morning, Contactman, Climber I, Climber II, and Sawman I were feverishly cutting, hacking, and pulling at the debris on and around homes near the volunteer center. What little conversation existed was to ask for a tool or for help with a heavy tree branch, or to share a curse. Two young men quietly drifted into the group and were acknowledged by a nod. They worked for about half an hour and then left, their departure as inconspicuous as their arrival. Their visitation had no noticeable impact upon the group, because it was not a group in any organized sense. Four individuals were fiercely working in intimate contact, but their interaction was minimal and incidental to the task of attacking the mounds of debris around them. Climber I recalls:

> My arms were aching quite a bit, because I hadn't used an ax in a long time. But I didn't care. It was worth it to see the chips fly.

Climber II later noticed a long scratch on his forearm and wondered how or where he had gotten it. Contactman remembered

feeling exhilarated by the hard physical activity, and pleased by the fact that I was sweating profusely . . . almost the same kind of feeling one gets when, after a period of nervousness before a football game, he charges into the game and plays hard . . . I was using a small saw for some time, and suddenly I discovered I couldn't release my grip on the handles; my hand had cramped into a clenched fist.

Sawman I had noticed that "rather than let the tools do the work, we were in there bending our backs and working harder than necessary."

The opportunity for uncomplicated and physically difficult labor—particularly when the work served in some way to "fight back" at the tornado's awesome damaging power—was cathartic for the crew members. Rigger, who joined the crew the second day, remembered

the work felt good. It felt the way I have wanted to feel, and I could allow myself to respond to the whole range and texture of feeling that I have denied myself since the tornado.

"Attacking" the debris was, for the crew members, a way of testing their capacities, of asserting power, and of redefining destruction they could not stop into destruction they could, in some way, control. Their "irrational," disorganized, and unsystematic battle with fallen tree limbs matched what to them was "irrational," disorganizing, and wanton tornadic devastation.

The activities on the first day may be seen as essentially cathartic. Each person worked alone, but nonetheless there was something comfortable about working in the presence of like-actioned others, even if names were not exchanged and verbal communication was minimal. Sawman I commented:

If I had been working all by myself, I would have felt kinda foolish, maybe, trying to do something alone with all that mess. Having the other guys there made me feel sort of stronger, I guess.

Contactman was reminded of "the fear you sometimes feel when standing watch alone on a black night at sea—a fear that vanishes when you remember there are unseen shipmates around you." Membership in the crew, particularly during the first day, provided a channel for catharsis and a comfort, through the proximity of others.

In the early afternoon, the crew members hurriedly ate lunch —sandwiches and coffee from a roving Salvation Army van— and returned to work. About an hour later Contactman, trying to find larger handsaws, walked the short distance back to the Volunteer Center. A bright yellow Civil Defense power wagon, rigged with an A-frame winch, was parked in front of the center. Contactman found its driver, and the crew core membership was expanded by one.

The presence of the power wagon had a marked impact upon the crew. Since all members could ride in or on it, their scope of operations was increased beyond walking distance. The truck had several compartments filled with useful tools, cables, and ropes, and it carried an extension ladder. With its A-frame winch, the wagon could lift or drag tremendous chunks of debris—far beyond the group's individual or collective strengths. Quickly baptized by the group as the Monster, the machine and its driver, "Monsterman," became part of the crew's cathartic activity. Roper II, who would join the crew the next morning, commented:

I felt that, like working in the crew, the crazy machine was at least partially an equalizer to the damage that had been done. I think that's what we felt, all of us—that singly, what the hell, a tree on a guy's porch is more than a match for us; but given this piece of equipment we could, instead of working with helpless anger, pull those goddam trees out of the way and get them off people's houses and porches.

This was an outlet to the helpless feeling that you have when you see so much desolation.

Contactman recalls:

It was very clear that the machine had been anthropomorphized by us and was really another member, a rather formidable member, of our work crew. When the Monster would be straining at a heavy load, we would shout encouragements to it and help it by tugging on ropes we had tied to the debris. When it was successful, and it always was, we would run over to it and pat it on the hood or slap it on the roof and fenders. I remember comments about the Monster lifting trees whose weight was beyond the winch's rated potential. I think we felt the Monster, like the rest of us, was being tested beyond its limits; it gave us confidence, somehow, in seeing it succeed.

The power truck provided the crew with a focus for a more organized sense of group identity. The members gradually arrayed themselves in functional work roles to the best utilization of the machine. Consequently, toward the end of the work day, a rudimentary division of labor began to develop. When a job was nearing completion, Contactman would scout in advance of the truck, spot homes endangered by debris, and speak with the owners about the crew's helping them. Monsterman drove the truck and operated the power winch. Climbers I and II scrambled on rooftops and up trees, setting the hook of the winch. Sawman I moved in with his power saw when rapid cutting was needed. Roper I, who had joined the crew late Friday afternoon, affixed guide or hauling ropes when necessary. If any member was not, at the moment, called upon to perform his specific work task, he would carry, clear, lift, or pull as the job demanded.

Though anonymity was still the practice there was markedly more verbal communication among the members as the afternoon wore on. This increased interaction was stimulated by the presence and performance of the Monster, by the experience of evolving and defining work roles, and by the decreased need for more isolated and personal vengeance upon the tornado. The hours of physical labor completed, the encouraging ameliorative power of the Monster had served to reassure and reorient, at least in part, threatened and confused individuals. Gradually, they were able to look beyond the haze of their own emotions to the individuals with whom they were working. The crew was reaching the point at which, as Rigger later interpreted, the members "were far enough removed from their initial response to the tornado that they could feel free to work together and be together and form a group together."

At 7:45 P.M. word got to the crew that he mayor had established an eight o'clock curfew in East Topeka. All volunteers had to be out of the area by that time. Monsterman protested, "But we're just getting going now. Why do we have to quit! There are some spotlights in the truck." Roper I complained, "We just start getting something done and some lousy regulation stops us." The group immediately discussed plans for "getting the same guys together tomorrow." The first hour generally agreed upon was 7:00 A.M., but because of transportation problems, the crew decided upon 8:00 A.M. Then, begrudgingly, they packed up and went back to the Volunteer Center.

As the sunburned, grimy, and sweaty crew members entered the center, they became aware of the striking difference in appearance between them and the volunteers inside the office. Looking at his own torn clothing and at his fatigued comrades, Climber I laughingly remarked, with pride and satisfaction, "We look more like disaster victims than volunteer workers." The startling contrast to, and attention and comments from, non-crew volunteers served to support group identity. The members separated for a few minutes, putting tools in a corner of the center, washing up, getting in line for food. However, one by one, they all went to the same table and began to talk excitedly about the challenges the day had brought to them, and how they and the Monster had met the challenges. The members teased one another about being "so out of shape that you won't show up tomorrow." After the meal, as the members were leaving, each polled the other, making certain of the time and place for meeting. It was agreed that if anyone were late, Contactman would leave word at the center's front desk of the crew's location, so the prodigal member could find, as Monsterman put it, "where he belonged."

THE SECOND DAY

By 8:30 Saturday morning, Contactman, Climber II, Roper I, and Monsterman had gathered their tools and were ready to go to work. Friday's other two core members, Sawman I and Climber I, had not yet arrived; and though there was discussion about waiting for them, the group decided to "leave word and shove off."

As indicated in Tables I and 2, three new core members joined the crew as preparations for work were being made: Roper II, Monster Assistant, and Sawman II. In addition to these, three other helpers—among them Roper II's young son—asked to come along and stayed with the crew for part of the day (all non-core crew members will be referred to as "ancillary" members.)

The crew had a particular location in mind when they loaded their tools and got into the Monster or Contactman's car. Toward the end of Friday, the crew had noticed a three-story house with an enormous fallen tree tangled in its peaked roof. The owner of the house had asked the crew to help him the next day, and they had agreed that it was "a job with real challenge."

Upon arriving at the site, the crew looked over the problem more carefully, trying to determine where to begin. The task was awesome. The tree was at least seventy-five feet high, had a trunk circumference of about six feet, and was heavy with twisted, broken, and dangling limbs. It had been blown onto the house with such impact that part of the wooden frame structure had moved an inch or two from the foundation. Most of the tree's roots had been ripped from the ground; the fractures of the trunk were such that the house itself seemed to be providing the major support for tons of tree. The crew was impressed by the danger of the job, and by the delicacy required to prevent further damage to the house. Bravado was set aside for the moment as the members made imaginary cuts here, winch pulls there, and calculated the angles of fall.

During these moments of planning, Sawman I arrived and was warmly welcomed by Friday's core members. "I was really afraid I wasn't going to be able to find you fellows," he said, and then, looking up at the tree, added, "God, you sure picked a winner, didn't you?" Rigger, the last of the core members, had also found the crew, was welcomed into their deliberations, and began verbally sketching a system of segmenting the tree into smaller chunks—from the top down—and lowering them by winch cable and rope, using the lower branches as booms and pulleys. The crew decided that the procedure was "worth a try," and to "give it hell!" Extension ladders were set, and the Monster was moved into position.

As the hours went by, the functional work tasks, the ephemeral roles, became sharper and more familiar to the enactors. Contactman contacted, Climber I climbed, Rigger rigged, Sawmen I and II sawed, Ropers I and II roped and guided, and the Monster tugged and lifted—*successfully*. Great pieces were cut from the tree and guided to the ground without further damage to the house. As each segment finally hit the ground, often after much straining and many "close calls," the crew members applauded themselves, the Monster, and the boom-pulley technique which had come to be institutionalized by the group as "Rigger's Law."

The cathartic activity of the day before was being shaped into role behaviors, and the associated expectations stimulated the evolution of specific positions within the group. The division of labor crystallized, and with it group cohesion and solidarity increased. The members, having pioneered a functional and successful niche in the crew, found their self-confidence being bolstered and their feelings of control over the environment reassured.

The activities of the crew—the men shouting to each other and scrambling in trees and on rooftops, the roar of the Monster's engine, the screams of the two power saws and the thuds of axes, the crash of falling branches—attracted the attention of some neighbors and passers-by. Though at this time there was little interaction between them and the crew, the presence of onlookers further fixed the group as an entity. If any member was asked who he was, he would identify himself as "a member of this work crew," and not by name or "civilian" occupation.

Late that morning, uniformed Boy Scouts—two men and three boys—joined the crew as ancillary members. As they came onto the work site, the scout leader, looking for an assignment, shouted to the crew members, "Who's the straw boss of this outfit?" Most of the crew members turned to look at the inquirers, but work continued. Contactman, who was the closest to being an informal foreman, set down the branch he was carrying with Roper II and explained to the Scouts, "We're a team; there is no straw boss." Monsterman Assistant added, "That's right! We've got too much to do. We haven't time for straw bosses!" With that introduction the scouts began helping to pile the fallen branches and to clear the yard. Though they worked hard—as hard as any core member of the crew—they remained alien to the group. Their uniforms identified them as members of another social order—the world "out there," the world beyond that which encapsulated the ephemeral roles. The scouts seemed quite satisfied with, and confident in, their customary pre-disaster role. Their very presence was an inadvertent attempt to impose that pre-disaster organization, confidence, and satisfaction upon the crew members—who wanted to evolve, and were evolving, their *own*. The Scouts wanted to know the typical social structure—where was the "straw boss"? The scout leader was puzzled that Contactman had not introduced himself as "a doctor at The Menninger Foundation"—a fact which the scout leader had learned from another ancillary member. Later, the scout leader suggested that "the crew split up, half stay at this place to finish up, and the other half to move on"—a sensible logistic suggestion that drew vehement protest from the crew core members. The scouts freely moved on, easily able to divorce themselves from the crew.

Never fully accepted by the crew, the scout's stay and the contrast they provided further defined group boundaries. At the same time, however, the scouts, highly formalized and smacking of secondary associations, were reminders that eventually the ephemeral roles would be phasing back into broader and more complex community roles.

At lunch time, the crew members got sandwiches and coffee from a Red Cross food truck near the work site and sat on the freshly severed chunks of tree while eating their meal. By then, some of the anonymity of the individual members had faded. The role moratorium was no longer complete. Many, but by no means all, of the core members had each other labeled by first name—the last names and "civilian" occupations (except in those few cases were core members had been acquainted before) remained largely unknown. What *was* clearly known by all was the functional work role, the ephemeral role, of each individual. Roper II observed: "We, you know, felt so close . . . I think we learned a way of working, you know, like the guy who could drive the Monster. There was the driver, and there was the guy who could kind of size up the situation, and another guy sort of assumed the task of talking with the people in the house. I think certainly very specific roles emerged that were quite appropriate to what we had to do. It's interesting, I still don't know the names of the guys. . . . It didn't seem important to ask. . . . It seems irrelevant." More bluntly, Sawman I commented about anonymity: "I felt like, well, I may not know his name, but I know that I can rely on him and that he ain't gonna drop this tree on me or something like that . . . the name wasn't important. . . . I didn't pay any attention to who the people were or what their status was in the community or anything like that . . . it didn't make any difference."

The anonymity in the crew was a reflection of the fact that proper names, as identifications in and links with a community-complex which was fractured and disrupted, had little meaning; in fact, served largely to remind the members of the disruption and of their own fears. Another identity—one based on a pioneered ephemeral role, which linked the member with comforting comradeship, growing competency, and a sense of control—seemed far more appropriate, at least for a time.

Though the ephemeral roles are discussed in this chapter as entities, they were not created *de novo*. They were the products of the experience, past and present, of the enacting human beings. Some accustomed modes of behavior—more on the first day than the second, and more on the second day than the third—were set aside by the individual for his own protection. Names and statuses were waived—dramatically so in the case of Roper II and Rigger, who had previously interacted as psychoanalyst and patient. As the ephemeral roles evolved further from their initial cathartic function toward more complex social behavior, other past experiences of the enactors became relevant. This phenomenon was especially manifest at lunch on the second day when the group members, most of them veterans, talked about the similarity of some of their military experiences with those in the crew. They talked about their "old outfits," and some of the "gang" they worked for or fought with. Humorous stories and tales of success under adversity were exchanged. The emphasis was upon aspects of the *informal* organization of the military and their similarities to the dynamics of the crew. Nonetheless, gradually the ephemeral roles were being broadened, similarities were being seen with other societal roles, pseudopods were being extended back into the *status quo ante*.

Though the crew's evolution was moving the members closer to a more typical social organization, they were not yet ready to accept formalization as such. After lunch, the crew returned to work, still at the site of the massive tree. Contactman went back to the center to check on the availability of plastic window and roof covers for the tornado victims. By this time, the center had become markedly more organized than the day before. Several other work crews were now in the field, and a dispatcher was responsible for their whereabouts. Contactman went to the dispatcher's desk, where he reported the location of the crew and received a list of names and addresses of people who had called in for help, or whose homes had been assessed by survey teams to be endangered by debris. Contactman was then given a pin and a cardboard badge proclaiming him to be a "Group Leader." He got the roll of plastic he had gone for and, outside the center, threw the badge into a trash container, later reflecting: "The badge seemed ridiculous . . . like wearing a necktie in a nudist camp. . . . If I were the group leader—and no one was really—it would have been known to the crew by my actions . . . not by a badge pinned on me by somebody back inside the center."

At 4:00 P.M., the crew had completed the job on the monstrous tree, and, with comments about *"being ready now for anything,"* the crew moved on to the addresses given to Contactman by the center dispatcher. The first two addresses did not exist, the third was a home completely flattened by the tornado, and the fourth had no tenants. Monsterman complained, "What the hell is with those people back at the center? Don't they know what's going on?" Sawman I advised Contactman to "throw away that damned list, and let's keep finding our own jobs." "We can't let this crew and the Monster go to waste," urged Rigger, and "we know better than anyone else what we can handle." The members agreed that the crew would operate autonomously, checking back with the center periodically for emergencies or "jobs that were worth a crew like us." All of the crew members were happy to be out in the field where they could "really help people," and not "back where all the red tape was." Of the ten core members, seven initially had associated themselves with formal organizations after the tornado, but were not satisfied either with the organization's response or with their own participation. They had found what they were looking for in the crew, and did not want it "fouled up by red tape."

The crew worked on several more houses before the 8:00 P.M. curfew. The jobs were not so dramatic as their first of that day, but still difficult, challenging, and, according to Monster Assistant, "The way we liked 'em." During this period there developed an unelaborate but noticeable argot and an increase in humorous exchanges among the members—both indexes of growing group solidarity. Monsterman had a seemingly inexhaustible supply of colloquialisms and, by his example, the tree being worked on became "that big sucker." Tools, ropes, the cable hook, or whatever was in demand at the moment became a "pea-picker," or "that pea-picking rope," or the like. Axes, were "tomahawks." The members kidded each other, particularly immediately before or after a difficult or dangerous act:

> Let it fall on your head, then it won't hurt anything! Don't worry about scars, you can't look any worse than you already do! Let's leave him up in the tree, he looks so natural there!

The humor might appear deprecatory, but was—by voice inflection, timing, and intent—quite supportive, and meant to tease a man out of his fear. Furthermore, the kidding, since it was of a personal nature and no one became angry, indicated the openness of the members to one another. There was also much general mirth associated with the crew's successes as well as with their mistakes. Contactman remembers, "Sometimes, especially at first, we must have looked like the Keystone Cops."

Toward the end of one of the afternoon's jobs Contactman, as was the pattern, left to locate the next job. Roper II accompanied him. Having found a house endangered by hanging branches and having talked with the occupants, Contactman and Roper II returned to the Monster—and it was gone! Contactman reports:

We were stunned by the fact that the Monster was gone, along with the rest of our work crew. The streets were a turmoil of trees, debris and equipment, and it was difficult to see the entire length of a block. We attempted to search the area by car, but still couldn't locate the Monster. We felt a sense of personal loss, and were genuinely concerned. Finally, after almost half an hour of searching, we spotted, on a street that had previously been blocked at both ends by other trucks, the ungainly but lovable shape of the Monster. The crew had moved to get out of the way of power company workers. We hurried to the Monster and our arrival was like the reunion of a family. We welcomed one another, and then started teasing each other about not being able to find our way around in an elevator. They had been looking for us, and we for them.

At lunch, the members had also demonstrated a feeling of solidarity and loyalty when they expressed concern about Climber I, who had not shown up for work that day. Sawman I, who had arrived a little late that morning, commented,

I was afraid that I was going to be late. I stopped to help some guy cut a little tree off his porch, and it took longer than I thought it would. I hurried, though, because I knew I had to get over to our crew. I didn't want to miss them!

The modal dynamics of the crew during the first day were individual and cathartic. Each member took comfort from the presence of the others, but interpersonal interaction among them was minimal. By the end of the second day, the members had "come out of themselves," and the group was the focus, and valued for itself. The modal dynamics of the second day were centered around the development of the group—the division of labor, evolution of ephemeral roles, increased interpersonal interaction, elaboration of argot and group humor, and intensification of core member loyalty to the crew. Rigger sensitively reflected upon these dynamics:

After some trial and error, the members of the crew found themselves accepting those particular jobs which seem to suit either their abilities or inclinations, and strangely enough, everyone seemed to have a place. . . . My own motives underwent some sort of metamorphosis as the group became more unified. *At first, I seemed to be concerned with proving myself* . . . in order to wipe out the frustration. . . . As time went on, though, this feeling changed substantially, particularly after the evolution of 'Rigger's Law.' . . . I found then that I took to the rooftops or tree-tops not as an exhibitionist, but out of an unfamiliar *sense of responsibilty for the group's success with each project.*

The crew finished its last job of the day about 7:45 P.M.—close to the curfew time. It had been a particularly dangerous problem, the tree crushing, and yet supported by, the front porch and roof of the house. The crew had moved the nine residents, including a man in a wheelchair, out of the building before going to work on it. Again, after considerable effort, the crew was successful. The tree, carefully trimmed of its broken branches, was manipulated away from the house, where it crashed safely to the ground. The members cheered, then noticed the hour and decided it was time to quit.

The decision to stop work was less difficult this night. The crew was at a good breaking point, having just "finished off a big sucker." They were tired; they had finished a dozen major jobs on this day alone, nearly twelve hours of labor, and some of the members had worked the day or days before. But contributing most to the acceptance of quitting time seemed to be that it had been a good day. The group, as Roper I expressed it, "was swinging." The other members, taking stock of the day's activities while packing their gear into the vehicles, agreed. Sawman I capped the discussion, "Well, there's no job we can't handle now—not after today!" Enthusiastically agreeing with Sawman I, the crew headed back to the Volunteer Center.

As on the night before, the physical appearance of the crew was in sharp contrast to the inside-office center volunteers. Now, however, there were more workers present from other crews. Also, as they had the night before, all the crew members sat at the same table, and again laughed and joked as they recounted the day's exploits and "close calls." Comparisons were made among jobs—techniques, unique problems, and so forth—a group history, task oriented, had accumulated and was being shared and re-inforced. As the meal continued, the crew decided that they would meet at the center the next morning by 8:00 A.M.—Sawman II still argued for 7:00 A.M.—with word left at the desk for late-comers. The members encouraged one another to be there. "We better show up," laughed Monster Assistant, "nobody else could stand to work with Monsterman." Sawman I, more seriously, commented, "It wouldn't be the same working in another crew." "Yeah!" Climber II amended explosively, "who else could make the Monster work miracles?"

During the second day two related phenomena emerged. The crew began to define more specifically the jobs they would under-take or not undertake, and they began to notice and comment upon the reaction of their "clients." These phenomena, indicating that the members were now starting to look beyond the group, would be central among the dynamics of the third day.

THE THIRD DAY

At 8:20 A.M., Sawman II, Roper II, Climber II, Monsterman, Monster Assistant, and Contactman left the Emergency Relief Center and went to their first job of the morning. Rigger and Sawman I, having checked at the center for the whereabouts of the crew, joined the rest about thirty minutes later and were warmly greeted. Climber I arrived shortly thereafter, explained his absence the day before. He had had to operate a bulldozer for his employers—had decided "it wasn't like working with the gang here,"—and was welcomed back.

Contactman recalls:

The group seemed a good deal more relaxed today, though we set about our tasks with the same, if not more, industriousness.

The crew efficiently completed four jobs in less than an hour— jobs that would have taken them an hour each the morning before, and which would have been impossible when the crew was first formed. Sawman I comments:

The third day, well, it just wasn't any work at all. It had become more or less a science by then.

The crew was working as a coordinated team around the Monster, and had become rather expert in the application of "Rigger's Law."

The crew had become increasingly selective about the jobs they would undertake. Though expectations were made especially when victims approached the crew for some special kind of help, generally "our kind of job" was a home: (1) hazarded by broken or felled trees of large size; (2) still inhabited by occupants who wanted help; and (3) where the crew would not "waste its precious equipment in minor jobs," or "waste manpower on small stuff the people could do themselves." The expertise of the crew was recognized and cherished by the members; they realized that the Monster was a rarity among equipment available for use on private property, and they preferred jobs which would maintain the division of labor and the ephemeral roles which they had evolved.

Contactman had been given a list of addresses that morning by the dispatcher at the center. When Contactman suggested to the crew that they go to some of those addresses, Monsterman complained, "Did you get that list from those guys back there who draw all the pictures and wave their hands back and forth in the air!" The crew laughed at this, and Contactman explained that the center had become quite organized, that their surveys were more accurate, and that his own earlier scouting indicated that some of the jobs on the list really were "worthy of our group." The crew then began to accommodate itself to some of the center's scheduling, but still insisted that, as Rigger emphasized, "We go our own way if we see people who want and need the kind of help we can give." Nonetheless, the ties between the crew and the center—which in turn was enmeshed with the community-wide disaster effort—were becoming stronger. On this third day, as a further example, the short-wave radio in Sawman I's panel truck, linked with the same radio circuit as the center, was used more than on the previous two days to inquire about legal, Red Cross, and Public Health aid for victims; and to ask for tools and equipment for the crew or for food, clothing, candles, plastic storm windows, and so forth for people in need. The crew was moving in the direction of increased specificity of purpose and increased formality. It was more closely approximating and articulating with secondary associations in the community social complex.

The crew's increasing awareness and evaluation of "clients" was another indication that they were expanding their attention beyond themselves as individuals and beyond the crew. Sawman I recalls that Sunday was

> the first time when it had really gotten through to me, when I paid attention to the people relying on us to do the work. . . . The crew was just finishing up one house and was going to move next door. I went over there and plunked my fanny down on the porch to rest for a minute and to work on my saw. . . . I got to talking to the people on the porch, and this was the first I had thought about what they were like, those people we helped.

The need for solitary catharsis had abated. The group was solid, the ephemeral roles were comfortable, predictable, and automatic, and the work had become more systematized and routinized. Satisfied with himself and satisfied with the crew, the core member was ready to look afield. He noticed the degree of gratitude and ingratitude among the tornado victims he helped. He complained about a few instances of exploitation or "being ordered around" by house owners. He became angry at some "big, healthy guys parked on their butts drinking beer while we worked on their houses," and at "that idiot who took movies of us up in his tree instead of helping us." He was touched by "the old lady who cried when we had to cut down the remnants of a tree 'that grew up with the children,' " and by the impoverished family that offered to share with him what they had for their evening meal—a few Red Cross sandwiches. Bit by bit, the crew member, armed with returning confidence, was opening himself to the broad spectrum of his pre-disaster experience.

Late that afternoon, the crew was proceeding to 123, an address given them by the Volunteer Center dispatcher, and specified as "a place needing a power winch to move a large tree trunk from a house." As they drove a circuitous route around blocked streets toward 123, they encountered one of their counterparts from the center—another volunteer work crew—also driving to some new destination. Enthusiastic greeting and brief tales of exploits were exchanged. "Where are you headed?" the other crew inquired. "To 123," the crew responded. "What!" protested the other crew. "We were just there, and did a damned good job too!" The hackles were raised as two crews—both proud of their accomplishments, and perhaps both evolved through the same dynamics—brushed in competition. Contactman made haste to explain that the crew was going to 123 to remove a tree trunk from a house, because "we have the Monster here." "Oh, that's different!" came the response from the other crew. "We trimmed it all off, but couldn't move the trunk. We got it all ready for you. Good luck!" Laughter again was shared, and there were hearty farewells. Both crews, assured of their integrity, moved on toward their respective destinations.

East Topeka was, even more than the day before, a mass of public utility workers—gas, electric, light, water, road, and telephone service vehicles and equipment edged through the streets, their modern machines clearing, repairing, and reconstructing wherever they went. In the midst of all this efficiency and power, the crew became increasingly aware of their ultimate obsolescence. The "pros" were moving in.

On their way to 123, the crew was stopped by a property owner who asked if they would "please cut that branch off up there that's dangling over where my kids like to play." The branch was beyond reach of the crew's extension ladder, the tree appeared unclimbable and inaccessible, and none of the members could throw a rope that high. As the crew pondered whether the limitations of their equipment would allow them to help, a United States Forest Service bucket truck came down the street; it was stopped by the crew, and the Rangers agreed to go up in the bucket and sever the threatening limb. Contactman recorded,

> The forest ranger was lifted with ease by the bucket apparatus and, with quick dexterity and a special trimming power saw, clipped down the dangling branch and several other potentially dangerous limbs in only a few minutes time. All of our crew stood watching the operation in awe. That job would have taken us almost an hour—if indeed, we could do it all—and the whole while we would have been sweating out ways of manipulating the falling branches away from the house so they wouldn't do any damage.

Roper II remarked,

> Look at that guy; he's dropping those branches at the bottom of the tree like stacked cordwood. He's *almost* as accurate as we are.

"Well, they may be able to do it faster," argued Sawman II, "but it's a lot easier for them than it was for us. We can be proud of what we did!" Rigger added, "They do a good job, but they don't do a *human* job." Monster Assistant laughed, "It looks as though automation is going to put us out of a job!" The ephemeral quality of the crew was made quite clear to the members, as was the competence and efficiency of a formal organization. This competence and efficiency, which might have been disrupted by the tornado, had now, for all members to see, returned.

The crew laughed at their "obsoleteness," took comfort in the fact that they had been "pioneers," a "crew with a soul," and "the first in the area, before all those fancy tools," and agreed "there's still lots of work we can do without that kind of equipment." They then continued toward the task waiting for them at 123.

At 123, the crew plotted the crosscuts to be made, and the rope and cable strains to be taken, in order to remove the large tree trunk wedged into the side of the house. The decisions were made, the techniques applied, and within less than twenty minutes "that big sucker" was on the ground. A single shingle was the only additional damage to the house during the removal process. The crew cheered itself, and Sawman I proudly exclaimed, "Hell, what's left for us now?" But as the crew members eyed the ominously darkening skies and felt the wind quicken, those words seemed less than indomitable.

The crew moved off in search of another job. Spotting the crew they had met on their way to 123, the Monster crew decided to "handle the big stuff" on the lot where the other crew was working. Both crews labored side by side, but did not merge, for about thirty minutes—often exchanging brief comments about their earlier activities. At 6:30 P.M. the other crew "knocked off and left the area."

The weather was getting heavier, and the members could see lightning rapidly approaching from the southwest. While Climber II was digging through Sawman I's truck for an ax, the shortwave radio crackled a storm watch for the Topeka area. The mayor used the circuit to discuss with other disaster officials what to do in the event of a tornado siren alert. When Climber II relayed the information to the crew, the members squared with a dilemma. They were halfway through a hazardous tree; they decided, "We have to finish it, or we'll leave it more dangerous than we found it." With thunder and lightning all around them, the crew worked frantically in the rain to get through the tree. The axes seemed dull and the saws terribly slow. Climber II, who had taken station by the radio, bellowed, "The military is moving out of East Topeka; one of their men got hit by lightning." The crew worked even more furiously—now not for catharsis, but from fear. Finally, the tree fell to the ground, precisely where the crew had planned it to fall, and they moved in to segment it further. Climber II screamed, "The center has ordered us out of here—there has been an unconfirmed tornado touch down just south of Topeka!" Contactman advised, "That's all. Let's get out." While crew members hurriedly loaded up their equipment, they expressed concern for each other's safety and warned one another to "drive carefully" and "take cover if you see a funnel." After brief good-byes, the group fractionated and the members went off in several different directions—most to their homes to "look after the family." Spawned by one tornado, the crew had been hastened toward its demise by the threat of another that did not develop.

The group's interpersonal ties did not break easily, however. Sawman I, Rigger, and Contactman—strangers before the tornado —still see each other on occasion. During the interviews for this study, the members delighted in talking warmly about their comrades, the Monster, and the experiences of the group. All the interviewed members said that they would have liked to get the crew together again the week end following its disbanding, but somehow they "just couldn't work it out." The ephemeral roles were no longer functional—the crew members had done their job, and with their faith in themselves and in society renewed, returned to their pre-disaster community niches. The ephemeral roles were, now, only something to talk about or write about.

THE FUNCTIONS OF EPHEMERAL ROLE

Sudden disaster, as the Topeka tornado, can be disruptive both to the personality structure of the individual and to the social structure of the community. The ephemeral role, as conceptualized and presented in this chapter, serves to ameliorate both disruptions. It provides the enactor with an opportunity to reassert his coping abilities and to re-establish his trust in and dependence upon complex social organization. The ephemeral role—including its associated position in the *ad hoc* group—becomes an integral part of a larger emergency social system: a system developing during the hiatus when significant components of the *status quo ante* seem ineffectual. The ephemeral role is part of the social mucilage that maintains community cohesiveness in the aftermath of disaster.

The emphemeral role evolved over a three-day period from a vaguely defined member status in the crew into a specific and functional work role, which was clearly associated with a group identity. Although there is something a bit arbitrary about day-by-day categorization of indivdual and group behavior, certain individual dynamics and the group dynamics did indeed seem more pronounced on given days.

On the first day, the crew primarily provided the members with a channel for catharsis: catharsis in the comforting company of like-motivated and like-reacting others. The exhausting, over-compensating, and inefficient physical labor apparently had the desired abreactive effect, moving the enactor closer to emotional equilibrium and restoring, at least in part, his confidence that he could "do something" about the uncontrollable tornado. The social organization of the group on the first day mirrowed the egocentric qualities of member behavior. Though it was evolving, there was no "groupness" in the organized sense of the word, only a feeling of commonality born of mutual catharsis and a mutual moratorium on customary roles.

The second day saw the individual, now more sure of himself, concerned with the crew as an entity, involved with his comrades, and earnest about his role in cooperative efforts toward group success. His behavior was less egocentric and more groupcentric: he was willing to consider some of the world beyond his own skin, but not yet beyond the firming boundaries of the group. He was taking advantage of the opportunity afforded by the crew to shape an ephemeral role and try it on for size; to replace some of his more customary, but temporarily inappropriate or inoperative, pre-disaster social roles; and to test the trustworthiness and stability of social organization in general. The enactor was discovering that the ephemeral role fit his needs, and that its enactment bolstered his confidence in himself and in social order. The groupcentric behavior quickly evolved a division of labor and rapidly developed group-focused argot, humor, loyalty, history, and so forth. Increasingly, the crew was manifesting the typical characteristics of a "small group."

The third day revealed the member to be self-assured and secure enough in his ephemeral role to look beyond the crew; to expand his perceptual field to include his "clients," other work crews, and the sights and sounds of disaster aftermath that he had defensively tuned out before. The group structure, the membership characteristics of refined division of labor, delimited group goals, manifest expertise, routinized behaviors, and increasing ties with the center, approximated the pre-disaster secondary associations and formal organizations which had been disrupted but which had not, demonstrably, recovered. The ephemeral roles evolved from relatively undifferentiated cathartic activity to the point at which the enactor, already sensing the encroaching obsolescence of the crew for himself and for the community, could facilely phase back into the social complex *status quo ante.*

There was a primitive quality about the individual behavior and the social structure of the crew during the first day from which the evolution of the ephemeral roles began. The individuals appeared to act in a frantic, uncoordinated, even irrational manner, and there was little sign of collective organization among the members. The division of labor and individual competence did not come until later. Drayer, Cameron, Woodward, and Glass (1954, p. 23) addressed themselves to the psychological aspect of this phenomenon and observed that "disaster engenders a regression to 'primitive' fears, and demands primitive coping behavior." Furiously hacking at trees and hurling debris may be "irrational" and "primitive"; but it may also be functional—

providing the individual with a chance to externalize and expend anxious energies, to "get something done." Thrashing about may test his environment and define his capacities in a fashion similar to earlier developmental patterns of self-definition.

Regression to a primitive form of social structure may be similarly functional. In a seminal paper, Turner (1966, p. 11), has hypothesized that "the reinstatement of organic solidarity after failure in the division of labor, either because of external crises or internal breakdown, requires a period for enactment of mechanical solidarity, to create the continuing assurances upon which organic solidarity depends." A high degree of differentiation and a proliferation of specialized activities keyed by an elaborate division of labor, according to Durkheim (1947, p. 129), defines "organic solidarity." It is a solidarity based upon the functional interdependence of differences. "Mechanical solidarity," on the other hand, is more primitive and is based upon feelings of sameness rather than differences—upon a common consciousness or a sense of likeness with one's fellows.

Tornadic disaster profoundly disrupts, at least for a time, the organic solidarity of a community. Turner (1966, pp. 6–7) suggested that following catastrophe, "there is often a resurgence of mechanical solidarity, based upon the vital sense of shared sentiment among the victims and other persons directly or indirectly involved in the disaster." Speaking specifically about group reactions in disaster, he adds, "the momentary isolation of the individual and nullification of the division of labor when the impact is sudden and drastic sends the group back to rebuild solidarity from the beginning."

The crew dramatically demonstrated a return to more primitive group structures for the purpose of rebuilding. The feeling of commonality was first generated within the crew by the shared experience of members' cathartic activity: undifferentiated behavior in an undifferentiated group. There was the cradle for mechanical solidarity. But the crew, once the bedrock components of self-confidence and social structure had adequately been reaffirmed, evolved beyond mechanical solidarity. Over the three days a division of labor evolved within the crew, and with it a prototype organic solidarity—setting the stage for the ultimate obsolescence of the *ad hoc* group and the members' return to complex society.

Turner (1966, p. 11) emphasizes that mechanical solidarity must be *enacted* if it is to serve a regenerative function. "It is as if people felt called upon to make a display of solidarity and were not satisfied merely with taking its presence for granted. The period of conspicuous mechanical solidarity is not simply an event preceding the re-emergence of organic solidarity, but a necessary stage before the division of labor can be reimplemented." As suggested in this paper, what may be enacted are ephemeral roles, malleable enough not only to accommodate the initial need for mechanical solidarity, but also to support evolution through mechanical to organic solidarity—in a limited time span.

Ephemeral roles, then, and the processes of the *ad hoc* group, as described here, aid in the psychological recovery of the individual and the social recovery of the community following disaster. The needs and motives of the counter-disaster syndrome evolve through group process into socially relevant adaptations, and the vacuum of the role moratorium is filled by meaningful but ephemeral roles which are reknit into the ongoing identity.

CHAPTER FIVE

THE EPHEMERAL INSTITUTIONS

W
E HAVE TRACED the ways in which old
roles and norms were laid aside in the
aftermath of the tornado, and how for a
time there developed a new spirit of community cohesion. For a time the old ways
of doing things were replaced by ephemeral
roles and new groups as thousands of individuals contributed
in some way to the social need. Not only services were volunteered but goods as well: from thousands of trunks came clothing
and bedding; people offered their homes to strangers; and food
was contributed by supermarkets and by hundreds of individual
housewives. This outpouring of services and help is one mani-

109

festation of the post-disaster Utopia; it too has received a separate label, the "cornucopia phenomenon" (Wallace, 1956, p. 155).

The cornucopia phenomenon is a social asset, but it also poses a social problem—the problem of integration and delivery. Without some kind of larger coordinating mechanisms, some coordinating institutions, volunteers would only stand and wait; clothing would remain unused; some areas of town would receive a surplus of service while other areas would be deprived.

In Topeka, the social problem of integration and delivery was met by the development, within twenty-four hours, of a new and complex institution, the Volunteer Center. Several of these opened, the largest having a life span of nine days, the others closing after four days. Each served as a collection and referral point for disaster service, as a shelter and kitchen, and as a center for information collection and coordination. Manned entirely by volunteers, the centers were as ephemeral as the volunteer role. The life cycle of a volunteer center—its development, operation, and death; its form, and the functions it served—will be described in this chapter.

In one sense Topeka was unique: seldom are the volunteer helpers brought together by a highly visible institution which springs up overnight. It is more usual for such formal agencies as the Red Cross to operate their own emergency shelters. Yet the uniqueness of Topeka was more apparent than real. As we shall show in this chapter, the Red Cross shelters did not operate as if they were stable, well-planned arms of a formal agency; instead they acted as if they were ephemeral institutions, and their effectiveness bore no relationship to the formal emergency plans promulgated by the central office. Some observers went so far as to claim that the major contribution from the official Red Cross agency consisted of the Red Cross insignia on the door, some medical services, and a few items of equipment.

In this chapter we explore some of the reasons why new forms of organization are forced to develop, and why a formal, centralized, and bureaucratized agency like the Red Cross has difficulty in coping with the immediate aftermath of disaster. The shelter operation sponsored by the Red Cross is contrasted with the Volunteer Center. We suggest that bureaucratic agencies are likely to come into head-on collision with the counter-disaster syndrome, the Utopian mood, and the ephemeral helping roles which accompany disaster. This collision is the root cause for the widespread disenchantment with the Red Cross reported by many studies of disaster (Moore, 1958; Form and Nosow, 1958).

Perhaps it is necessary, however, to make one disclaimer in advance. This chapter focuses upon the immediate aftermath of the tornado, and upon the reports of volunteers who were struggling in unpracticed ways with novel tasks. It does not focus upon the longer-term needs resulting from the tornado—the continuing need of the victims for services and aid, money and support; the continuing need of nonvolunteer work crews for food and shelter—which the Red Cross did so much to meet. The volunteers were highly critical of the Red Cross as it operated during the short-term aftermath of the tornado; criticism of its long-term operations was rarely heard. Since this chapter is concerned with the short rather than the long term, it necessarily does injustice to the total Red Cross contribution.

THE GROWTH OF A VOLUNTEER CENTER

The development of the Volunteer Center can best be told through the experiences of Dr. Robert Harder, coordinator of volunteer efforts in Topeka. At the time of the tornado Harder lived in the low-income area of East Topeka. Trained to the Methodist ministry, he had served a year as a research associate with The Menninger Foundation and then became head of the local Office of Economic Opportunity Community Action Program. Thirty-nine years old, he had made a name for himself in civic affairs; he had helped organize a community betterment effort in a low-income section of Topeka, had served three terms as representative to the state legislature, and was a member of numerous community boards and organizations. Through these efforts Dr. Harder had developed a wide acquaintance in the community. He was known to politicians, minority group representatives, businessmen, social agency personnel, and people in the professional community. His formal and informal contacts thus gave him a wide-ranging communication network which could be quickly adapted to new tasks during the period of emergency.

When the sirens blew their warning on Wednesday evening, Harder left his OEO office and joined his family in their basement. His house was on the fringe and suffered little damage. Soon after the storm Dr. Jack Bremer, the minister of the East Topeka Methodist Church, a close personal friend, appeared. Together the two men set out to explore the damage. They moved slowly through the storm-ravaged areas of East Topeka, talking to a family here, helping remove rubble there. About midnight they encountered an ambulance driver who told them that the damage extended all over town. This came as a surprise; they had not listened to the radio since the initial impact and had imagined the disaster to be more limited. Harder knew from his prior experience that the nerve center of the rescue operations would be at Civil Defense headquarters. He and Bremer found their way through tree-cluttered streets and reached Civil Defense at 2:00 A.M.

There they found that plans "had already been pretty well laid for the cleanup." The immediate need was for a systematic search-and-rescue mission throughout the entire East Topeka tornado area; and Harder volunteered to take charge of the search. He had no experience in directing search-and-rescue missions, but the need seemed obvious. He was willing to take the responsibility, and the mayor and police chief were willing to delegate it. Forty airmen from Forbes Air Force Base, south of Topeka, were assigned to him, and by Thursday morning the search-and-rescue operation was under way. The search party completed its task about three o'clock Thursday afternoon: one body had been discovered, and the rescue crews realized with relief that the fatalities and injuries were less than anyone had dared to hope.

It was while this search was being conducted that the idea of a Volunteer Center developed. Said Harder:

> It seemed like the logical next step. It seemed obvious that beyond a search party another step was needed. The thought was to get people out on the streets and systematically go from door to door *offering* help.

The search had provided the raw experience which suggested the next social task.

After Harder concluded the search operation, the regional office of OEO phoned to offer financial assistance and the services of two hundred Job Corpsmen. This offer of help immediately presented organizational and structural questions. Who could manage the money? Who could direct and coordinate the Job Corpsmen? Through what structure could these services be related to other recovery activities? Harder promised to discuss the offer with the city officials and give OEO an answer the next day.

That night Harder ate supper at the home of a friend, a clinical psychologist. Having been forty hours without sleep, he did not remember this conversation in much detail, but the results were clear. With his friend, Harder discussed ways that local volunteers and OEO assistance could be integrated to meet the tasks of recovery (see pages 136–37). From that conversation came the idea of a series of Volunteer Centers, each center offering a comprehensive set of services under one roof. Later that evening, Harder proposed the idea to the mayor at a strategy-committee meeting in Civil Defense headquarters. The mayor agreed to the plan and appointed Harder coordinator of volunteer efforts.

Several goals for the Volunteer Center emerged. The first envisioned a reaching out of help: "We wanted to get people out on the streets to talk to victims who were still dazed from the impact of the storm. We wanted to help them get started if at all possible." As a second goal, a comprehensive group of services was to be offered. "We wanted to provide the full range of services within each center, i.e., legal aid, clothing, food, signing up for Red Cross help, housing information, case finding: a focal point for volunteer workers, and a place where people could come for help in cleaning up their yards and moving from one house to another." As a third goal, "There was need for a corps of volunteers to work on the private cleanup. So we started drawing in volunteers to do this."

The rest of Thursday night Harder used his contacts and knowledge of resources to begin "conning people out of stuff like the civil defense radio," but it really did not take much conning to get help—"actually everyone was cooperative." Bremer volunteered the use of his church's fellowship hall as headquarters of the volunteer effort. A friend of Harder's volunteered to get the kitchen in the fellowship hall organized and in use. Simon Martinez, then assistant director of the Topeka OEO, procured tables. Another friend became general manager. Most of the services were mapped out before Harder left the center for a morning press conference at the governor's office. By the time he had returned to the center at 12:30 P.M. the place was humming with a full range of services in operation. A call for volunteers was sent out. The principal of East Topeka Junior High School assumed the job of coordinating work crews. Things seemed to mushroom: kitchen help and facilities, food, clothing, legal aid, work crews, and social services were quickly set up.

Once things were started, Harder "stepped back and largely let it run itself." The center evidently met a major need; its usage was heavy for a week after the tornado. Red Cross workers talked to victims in one corner of the room, while in another corner "social work" volunteers returned to report the results of their house-to-house canvasses to a chief social worker. Work crews reported on work completed and picked up other assignments. Kitchen crews prepared food and cleaned tables while

"It was coming at a pretty good clip, two or three blocks wide, and all of this debris coming out of the side of it. It had a gray, heavy-rain look. . . ." (*Photo courtesy of* Topeka Capital-Journal)

Men and equipment arrived from as far away as Tennessee, and from all over the Midwest. (*Photo courtesy of* Topeka Capital-Journal)

A luxury apartment complex lay in ruins. (Photo courtesy of Topeka Capital-Journal)

Red Cross feeding units provided hot food and cold drinks for weary victims and volunteers. (Red Cross photo by Palmer)

tornado victims ate. Clothing, blankets, and furnishings were brought into the building, sorted by volunteers, and given to victims—or to people who were assumed to be victims. Sheets of plastic, nails, and tools were brought to the center and distributed to field crews. Two telephones rang incessantly. The Civil Defense radio stood on a table near the phones; it occasionally broke into a raucous call for something or someone, giving a sense of heightened emergency and tension. Angry tones were mixed with solicitous ones as sympathy warred with frustration and lack of sleep. It seemed impossible for one fellowship hall to contain so much activity.

Two other Volunteer Centers were established, one at Central Congregational Church in midtown, the other at Community Baptist Church in southwest Topeka. These two centers functioned largely as sites for gathering and dispensing information, but they never had the total range of activities which characterized the East Topeka operation. Occasionally they gave counseling to someone who wanted to know about services available from the Red Cross, Salvation Army, or Small Business Administration. Most of these limited informational needs were quickly met, and within three or four days the two smaller centers were closed. But the larger East Topeka center continued in operation for nine days after the tornado.

What did the Volunteer Centers offer that could not have been offered by the conventional disaster agencies? Did the establishment of Volunteer Centers simply rob Peter to pay Paul? Were resources drained from the Red Cross and the Salvation Army that might have been used more efficiently and with less confusion? One answer is given by Harder's comment:

> I feel that the traditional agencies have traditional approaches. There were some unique things that we did in our emergency centers that were not being done by either by the Salvation Army or the Red Cross; we made a quick attempt to get people out on the streets—talking to people in their home and providing them with information. No

one else was doing this in the same systematic way that we tried to do it. There wasn't any other agency that was offering the full range of services all under one roof as we were trying to do in East Topeka. Also, other agencies do not make any special effort to work with people in the clean-up of private property. A Volunteer Center certainly gave a home base for a large number of people who wanted to work. I think that is important. We operated under a philosophy of generous giving and not accountability. Because the Red Cross is institutional, they have to do more record keeping than we had to do as a volunteer operation, and I think record-keeping slows down the generosity of any kind of agency.

As a local board member of the Red Cross said:

Bob took upon himself a situation—which frankly I doubt that I would have had the courage to do, because he had literally put his arms around the whole community as a volunteer—where, with a different outcome, he could have been subject to fantastic criticism. . . . Harder, to the [Red Cross] executives who didn't know him, was sort of like a "wild-eyed demander" getting things done, and had no understanding of how the Red Cross worked.

But this is only one side of the story. At the other extreme some people questioned the entire legitimacy of the Volunteer Center:

Let me say this in reference to the growth of the volunteer service—that from the standpoint of the Red Cross it had some effect on the slowness of people in recognizing the Red Cross as *the* emergency and rehab long-term program group. . . . I think if there is to be such a thing as this again, there has to be much closer coordination with the *reliable* and *responsible* agencies in reference to the services to be rendered for these people. Let's face it, the more spoons in the broth the quicker you can spoil it, because everybody's taste bud is a little bit different.

Or, as another agency official commented:

> I think there are also some questions raised as to whether or not this whole plan for a Volunteer Center had been clarified with the Red Cross. Red Cross is the *responsible* agency in the disaster. I don't know, but there have been some comments since about lack of clarification of responsible agency.

What emerges from such remarks is a sense of conflict between the Volunteer Center, an ephemeral institution, and the formal, stable, bureaucratic organization as exemplified by the Red Cross. The ephemeral institution embodied the values of the post-disaster Utopia; it emphasized the role of the unspecialized volunteer, the desire for maximum flexibility, the impatience with record-keeping and accountability, and the emphasis upon a personalistic transaction between victim and helper. On the other side was the Red Cross, a formal organization which embodied the values of stability, legitimacy, specialization of role function, social accountability, and formalized rules and regulations.

THE RED CROSS SHELTER: AN INSTITUTION EPHEMERALIZED

Unlike the Volunteer Center which mushroomed overnight, the Red Cross shelters developed from a standing plan for shelter organization in disaster:

> The Red Cross has set up a very lively volunteer group to look after problems of shelter. . . . They have another group which is supposed to get food, prepare it, deliver it and serve it. Another group is responsible for registration information—who people are, what damage they sustained, their injuries, their financial housing and clothing needs and what have you.

Responsibility in the Red Cross is thus subdivided with the expectation that in disaster these various groups will function in a coordinated fashion, all working from a single shelter.

The development of a Red Cross shelter provides a contrast to the development of the Volunteer Center in East Topeka. For people already involved with the Red Cross, disaster resulted in mobilization of existing roles. One member of the shelter committee was at Red Cross headquarters by eight o'clock Wednesday night:

> I stayed there about forty-five minutes to get the reports from the survey groups so we had some idea what was going on, and what we needed to be prepared for. The survey team started in the southwest corner of town, so all the data we got in an hour and a half was what the survey team found in the southwest.

From these survey reports an initial plan was developed. Since the information was incomplete, shelter plans were made for only one area of town, the relatively prosperous west side. It was only by the next day that awareness of the total impact developed.

The shelter group thus decided to set up shelters in two schools, McEachron Elementary and Jardine Junior High School. Arriving at Jardine, they found the principal there already:

> Jardine was a beautiful place, would shelter people with a lot of space. But the principal pointed out that Bishop Elemeltary School looks right down on the damaged area. They had water and everyone was congregating there.

On the spot, the shelter team decided to use Bishop School as the Red Cross shelter. This was a fortunate decision, for when the group arrived at Bishop School they found that a first aid station had been set up by a separate Volunteer Red Cross team. It would have been quite possible for the shelter operation to be in one school and the medical operation in another; the informant guessed that the matter had not even been discussed at the central office. By the time the shelter group arrived the shelter was in fact set up; the school principal, the head of the Parent-Teacher Association, the school secretary, and the school engineer had arrived on their own initiative to open the building and show people the available facilities; three women volunteers were registering victims and getting information. In fact, things went especially well because the volunteers had come with a pre-existing knowledge of the neighborhood. They knew the disaster victims, and they did not have to start from the beginning. Later that evening the Red Cross delivered fifty cots. That night, into the morning, the shelter team spent their time registering people.

That first evening, the people who sought the shelter seemed in reasonably good spirits. Later that night "a lot of people started showing up from Kansas City and Wichita and so on— people who had a sister or a relative in the disaster area. The rest of the evening was spent in working with these people."

The Red Cross plans had anticipated that there would be many homeless who would seek shelter. In fact, no one really wanted to stay at the shelter, and only a dozen or so settled down for the night:

The rest had friends that they stayed with. Some felt their home was safe enough, even though the roof was gone. They weren't going to stay in any mass shelter. I guess that would be true in most disaster situations.

The experience of the first evening provided a prologomena to the remaining days of the shelter operation. It was not, in any real sense, a shelter at all. The next night it was used for sleeping by only one person—an inebriated woman who had fought with her husband—and she was from an area undamaged by tornado. People did not want to stay in the shelter. Instead it became a focal point for disaster-related activities. "What you need is a feeding operation and a registration point right after a tornado. You need a place where everybody who is working in the area can get communications." The functions of the shelter thus developed in response to unanticipated neighborhood needs.

Surprisingly enough, as it developed the shelter operation relied very little upon services or know-how provided directly by the Red Cross. Most of the work and supplies came informally from volunteers. One man described the operation as he found it at eight o'clock the morning after the disaster:

> The generator was there and running. They had a string of lights that went through the front door around the desk and right into the medical aid station. They had about a dozen cots in the aid station. And then in the large gym area they had fifty cots set up. In the other half of the gym, the tables were set up where they were eating. There were stacks of extra cots and extra blankets there. There was no refrigeration and that was our first concern, because milk was sitting around and so was food. The food was not from the Red Cross; several of the stores had brought out food and perishables. A refrigerator was hooked into the generator circuit but more plugs were needed so we had to go out and buy our own. I gave some money out of my pocket. It was strictly volunteer help at that time except for the medical people. We had no communications, the phones were out. When I got there the only person who stayed on from the night crew was one gal, and she was more or less running the show. We started to register people. It was very fortunate that we were in a school because they have a lot of equipment all ready for that kind of thing. I went down to check the kitchen and the young girl there was a volunteer. She said she wanted to stay, and I said okay as far as I am concerned you are running the place. She couldn't have been more than a senior of high school age.

Activity was uncoordinated—the shelter was manned by volunteers—yet seemingly effective nonetheless. Food was donated by individuals and by the Red Cross—"We were getting sandwiches but we kept running out of things like coffee." Finally the Red Cross sent people to the shelter to inventory the requirements:

> They told me to "Let us know what you want," which I did. And then we never saw or heard from them again.

Although some food was forthcoming, it was not adequate to the needs. The Red Cross sent fifty cans of mustard, but this was not very helpful. Finally one volunteer took on himself the task of gathering food:

> He said, "I'll go house to house in the neighborhood and start getting food for you." . . . He did a tremendous job. In fact, it was almost too good—Friday afternoon we started getting all kinds of food. There were baked beans and prepared food, more than we had the facilities to handle. By Friday, older women in the neighborhood started coming in and volunteering and they took over the kitchen. And then all through the rest of the day and all through Saturday people came in with baskets of prepared food.

In other words, the Red Cross shelter was finding the same source of supplies and operating in much the same fashion as the Volunteer Center in East Topeka. Help and coordination from the central agency was notable only by its absence.

This lack of central agency help occasioned no distress at the East Topeka center because no one expected it to be otherwise—it was not after all an official representative of anyone. But at Bishop School, where the personnel were supposedly representing the Red Cross, it was a different story. Here the lack of coordination and facilities led to irritation and disappointment:

> People wanted trucks. So we would go and call down by radio to Red Cross headquarters. And they would say, "We'll see what we can do for you." You would be talking to some radio operator but you couldn't talk to anybody with authority; you weren't talking to the guy who was handling vehicles. Well maybe the guy would show up two hours later with the wrong kind of truck. Friday I tried for three hours to get hot coffee. On Saturday a beam fell on a kid and one of the doctors thought his spine might be affected. He said we needed an ambulance. For two hours we tried to get an ambulance for the boy. We called the Red Cross. Finally at four o'clock Saturday afternoon an Air Force lieutenant showed up to coordinate things. I told him

we wanted medical help . . . and I pointed to the guy lying over there in the cot. I said we had been waiting two hours for an ambulance. About fifteen minutes later an ambulance came in from Forbes Air Force Base. So for food and everything else it was just a matter of scrounging.

Coupled with this growing irritation were small symbolic acts which made the situation even more difficult:

> Finally the Red Cross people did come out. They posted a lot of signs that said, "Here is what your Red Cross can do, . . ." They put up Red Cross posters and everything. And then a photographer came to take pictures of the Red Cross in action.

To the volunteers this was adding insult to injury. As one man said, "We were running [the shelter] in the name of the Red Cross, but you felt like you were no more part of Red Cross than you were of the Greek Orthodox Church."

Another similarity between the Red Cross shelter and the Volunteer Center emerged: the people in the Red Cross shelter quickly decided that an outreaching kind of service was more appropriate than a centralized service. Although the Red Cross had mobile canteen units which could stop in a neighborhood with side panels open and distribute food and coffee, relatively little use was made of them or of the central kitchen at the school:

> We could see by Friday that a lot of people would not come in to eat. They were so anxious to get their homes covered or get their furniture moved. So when some Girl Scouts volunteered I said, "Can you get cars?" They said they could get their mothers to drive. So we had four cars out that we loaded up with food. We painted big signs with the school materials to stick on their car—"Food and Drink." So they took food out and drove up and down.

As one informant suggested, this reluctance to come to the shelter perhaps reflects a more general pattern:

I'm not sure that in the normal course of life people want to go to some central point to get things. Everybody begrudges the fact of having to go down to the county courthouse to get their license tags. Most of us handle it all by mail if we can.

It thus appears that the Red Cross shelters developed in response to the same social forces that governed the growth of the Volunteer Center: the emphasis upon outreaching helping activity; the reliance upon the cornucopia as a means of obtaining food and service; and the use of volunteers, not on the basis of their ascribed role but on the basis of willingness and visible ability. There was even the same impatience with bureaucratic impedimenta:

A woman came in to talk to people about how to fill out forms. I asked her if she could help us if the people needed money or if the people needed housing. She said, "No, I can't help you in any of those things." So far as I could see she was only there to register. She set up a little office.

For most of the shelter staff, the emphasis was upon doing, not upon procedures.

However, the official Red Cross did have the decision-making power, and certain of these decisions had strong impact. The volunteers in the Red Cross shelter found themselves battling the central office:

We got the order that they were going to close this Bishop School. They were going to move to Jardine because that school had better kitchen facilities. Jardine is three quarters of a mile out of the disaster area at least. So I got on the radio to the Red Cross and they said "We can't help it. We're going to close you down."

Finally, after some argument, the decision was rescinded. But the source of final decision remained a mystery:

Who is making these decisions I have no idea. There seemed to be a total lack of chain of command.

Other problems arose too, reflecting a similar lack of coordination:

As the days went by there was a growing conflict between the medical personnel and the shelter people. The conflict was mainly about supplies and medical responsibility. Yet the shelter people are not supposed to supervise medical personnel.

One volunteer worker went so far as to say that the lack of coordination between the Red Cross groups duplicated the disaster. In the Red Cross, as in the tornado path, social relationships were disrupted and the coordinated structures of society were shattered. In the central Red Cross there was seen to be "a great concern about power structure and who was responsible for making decisions. There was a problem of people saying, 'That's not my job.' "

In short, it would be a mistake to think of the ephemeral institution as a unique kind of structure. The shelter at Bishop School operated much like the Volunteer Center in East Topeka during its brief life—it made use of the same resources; it responded to the same drives; and it was governed by the same values of the post-disaster Utopia.

The experience of the Red Cross in Topeka was not unique. Over the past fifteen years different reports show the same syndrome of behavior.[1] The local Red Cross organization has paper plans that function poorly or are not related to the realistic needs of the emergency period. The immediate post-disaster tasks are met instead by ephemeral volunteer groups. The procedures imposed by the Red Cross and its failure to provide immediate services leaves a residue of criticism and conflict. Our impression in fact is that the criticisms and conflicts in Topeka were more

---

[1] Form and Nosow, 1958, chap. xii; Wallace, 1956, pp. 145–46; Barton, 1962, pp. 237–63; Moore, 1958, pp. 176–80.

constructive and less continuing than in most other disasters reported in the literature.

BUREAUCRACY AND CRISIS

Such observations lead inevitably to a more general question. Why does the spontaneous volunteer organization seem to arise as a separate institution when such activities are really a legitimate task of the disaster-ready organizations? To answer this question requires a consideration of the nature of the Red Cross, and of the task with which it is confronted.

The Red Cross is a bureaucracy. This term is not used as an epithet; bureaucracies exist because they provide an efficient way of accomplishing certain kinds of organizational tasks. Bureaucracy is simply a way of subdividing larger goals so that each person or work unit can specialize. A bureaucracy is analogous to a factory, in which different workers specialize in particular limited tasks. The factory or the bureaucrat worker is usually trained for his job; he receives certain rewards and honors as his due, is seen as the "legitimate" person in his area of competence, and operates according to a clear set of rules and regulations. As Merton (1957) has pointed out, the bureaucratic structure also can be dysfunctional. Formal procedures may lead to depersonalized relationships between people. Rules and regulations may come to have a secondary autonomy of their own, so that inflexibility and conformity appear. Bureaucracy also may breed a type of jealousy: with specialization may come an increased sense of self-importance, and a tendency to value expertise in small things at the expense of total organizational functioning. This is only natural, since the over-all tasks of the organization may seem distant and outside the control of the bureaucrat, while his specific subtask is clearly his responsibility. With the growth of specialization the way is open for disruptive infighting and the jealous guarding of prestige.

Such dysfunctional processes are perhaps not of great importance in situations in which the bureaucracy deals with tasks which are stable and continuous. Strains are apt to become apparent however when the organization is suddenly confronted with entirely new tasks and new demands. Such is the typical dilemma of the Red Cross. In times of emergency the Red Cross finds itself caught in crisis—the stable and continuing tasks change overnight, and new tasks and demands clamor for attention.

When disaster strikes, the community is strongly affected by the utopian mood. There is great emphasis upon the immediate giving of help; the community becomes energized toward the emergency tasks confronting it. Traditional social roles are put aside. The important thing in disaster is not what one is, but what one can do. As we have seen, during the crisis phase the Red Cross was not organized for flexible action—perhaps no bureaucracy could be. It had its procedures and programs; unhappily these were not always appropriate to the emergent and shifting tasks of disaster.

The Red Cross workers were also seen as ineffective. They came with starched uniforms and a sense of self-legitimacy. They were, after all, the responsible agency and represented the "official" help. The volunteer workers took a very different view. They had no preconceived notion of how they "should" act or react. Squabbles and anger resulted.

We have shown earlier how the volunteers easily became impatient with Red Cross workers. This impatience was reciprocated by the agency personnel. The resultant strain extended to all levels of organizational interaction. One man on the Red Cross board was caught in the middle; he acted as a buffer between the personalistic operations of the volunteer organization and the institutionalized operations of the Red Cross:

> Most of my work involved keeping the Red Cross and the volunteer organization from a head-on collision. I had loyalties to the volunteer organization, but it seemed to me at times that the volunteer workers were fantastically unreasonable to a group of people who had come here from all

over the country. People with know-how came. Volunteers just can't dispense all of the money. Red Cross brought in their caseworkers and experts to help. On the other hand, you can see that Bob [Harder] and his workers were looking at the good of the victims on a highly personalized and individualized basis.

In the utopian period immediately following the tornado, bureaucratic procedures simply aroused antipathy and derision.

In short, the ephemeral institutions were the major vehicles for immediate emergency help. In one part of the city a new social agency arose to work with friends and neighbors; help was given within the social network of the neighborhood. In another part of the city, the ephemeral institution grew within the framework of the Red Cross shelter, yet was carried out by those who had access to the supportive and linking social ties which existed before the disaster. It was this native leadership, arising from debris and human need, that did the emergency work. It was only after the unique and short-term emergency was met that the bureaucratic organization could function and show its strength.

CHAPTER SIX

THE EPHEMERAL GOVERNMENT

T HE CITY, like a living organism, is a study in
systemic complexity. In their day-to-day activities people take the fruits of this complexity
for granted. The tap is turned and water comes
forth; the switch is thrown and there is light;
the road leads from an expectable here to a
predictable there—the complex interdigitation of function is so
commonplace and natural as to be invisible. But with disaster all
is changed, the system is disrupted, the organizational routines
are gone. Great and unexpected demands are made upon the
mechanisms of control, the facilities for repair, and all those institutions whose coordinated workings make existence possible

within that most artificial and contrived of organisms, the city.

If it is to survive disaster, the city must meet these unexpected demands, and meet them in a coordinated way. Population must be controlled and limits set. Victims and property must be protected, sightseers channeled into innocuous routes, and access provided into damaged areas. Public and semipublic property must be cleared and repaired. The victims must be given food, clothing, shelter, and medical care. Help must be available for the repair of private property. The needs must be surveyed, emergency plans developed, priorities assigned. Recovery efforts must be coordinated. Divergent agencies and groups must work together; new patterns of command, control, and communication must be found. As the crisis is new, so must the governmental response be new. The usual urban procedures of check and balance, of office routine, of scheduled work and division of labor, must be radically revised.

And in fact this is what happened in Topeka after the tornado. We may refer to this period of radical revision as the time of the "ephemeral government." Responding to the stimulus of disaster, different community leaders, ordinarily unrelated in any formal sense, came quickly together to plan, coordinate, and expedite effective action. From the pre-existing social matrix of informal contact, informal associations, and divergent agencies there emerged for a time an ephemeral governing structure, different in form, action, and capability from that which had gone before. Faced with new tasks, it developed new procedures and drew on new resources, only to disband when the period of crisis was ended.

Like anything constructed by human effort, the form of this ephemeral government was in part unique. Topeka and its specific needs called forth specific responses. But in part it was an example of a more general phenomenon, for the development of an ephemeral government is common after disaster. Thompson and Hawkes (1962) have used the phrase "synthetic organization" to denote the phenomenon. After reviewing many reports of disaster, they suggest that the community exists initially in what Lewin (1947) has called a "quasi-stationary equilibrium." When this equilibrium is disrupted, the resultant fragmentation and disorganization is halted by the development of a new governmental form. Temporary coordination and control emerge. As the crisis is met there follows a process of desynthesis, in which the synthetic organization is disbanded and control is returned to the usual institutions and routines.

To the student of urban society this rapid—indeed, radical —transmutation of government poses food for thought. In the normal flow of urban life the governmental structures appear monolithic, unyielding; change moves with glacial slowness. Yet under the unique stress of disaster the forms of government change almost instantaneously. What are the processes, what the roots, of this dramatic transmutation? What does it show about the regenerative power of human organization? We here approach these questions by analyzing the development of the ephemeral government, its formation, its social and psychological roots, and the processes which determine its form, function, and fate.

THE KEY UNITS

Although many people were involved in Topeka's synthetic organization, we shall limit our description to a few of the crucial actors: Charles Wright, mayor of Topeka; Darold Main, chairman of the Shawnee County Commissioners; Dana L. Hummer, chief of police of Topeka; Robert Jones, coordinator for Civil Defense in Topeka; Major General Joe Nickell, adjutant general of the state of Kansas; Dr. Robert Harder, then executive director of the Office of Economic Opportunity in Topeka; and William Avery, governor of Kansas.

On the evening of June 8, most of these men became immediately engaged in some activity which related to the approaching storm; but Mayor Wright had not been notified of the alert. He had gone to a meeting of a civic club on the northeastern edge of the city. Chief Hummer, who lives within 150 yards of the initial impact point of the tornado, had been called, and was talking to the police dispatcher as he watched the tornado approach. Jones was on his way to Civil Defense headquarters, having received an alert through his close connections with the weather bureau. General Nickell was in Manhattan, Kansas, inspecting damage to his men and equipment which had been caused by that tornado. Dr. Harder was at his office, preparing for a meeting of neighborhood officers, which was scheduled for seven o'clock that evening.

When the tornado hit, Chief Hummer drove directly to Twenty-ninth and Gage, near the initial impact point, and set up a command post. This was 7:05 P.M., and the funnel was still moving across the city. He kept in touch with his dispatchers, and with officers at various points on the route of the tornado, by using a two-way radio. Immediately he sent out a call for all off-duty personnel to report to stations, and the police department began a preliminary search-and-rescue operation.

At 7:20, Forbes Air Force Base, just south of Topeka, unable to reach the Civil Defense headquarters, contacted Chief Hummer. The Air Force agreed to send two hundred men to help control sightseers, looters, and traffic in the devastated area. By 7:30, command posts were established at several points along the tornado's path.

William H. Avery, then governor of Kansas, had been alerted through mass media, and went to Twenty-ninth and Gage to survey the damage. There he met Chief Hummer, and they discussed the probable need for the National Guard. Governor Avery used a two-way radio to contact General Nickell, who was returning from Manhattan, and asked him to report to the command post at Twenty-ninth and Gage. In the meantime, Commissioner Main, seeing debris flying by his window, went to Civil Defense headquarters, where he met Jones. The mayor had not yet arrived, and Main and Jones decided to call members of the county work crew, and to obtain tools and heavy equipment needed for removal of debris from the streets.

Mayor Wright was notified of the tornado at the club meeting. He immediately left for Civil Defense headquarters by automobile. En route, he saw the funnel pass the airport and move out of the city. Most of the direct route was blocked by debris, and after several detours the mayor arrived at Civil Defense headquarters at about 7:45 P.M. There, he tried to contact Topeka's four radio stations, but found that only one had two-way radio communication with Civil Defense headquarters. Mayor Wright broadcast to the citizenry on this station, pleading with them to stay at home out of the way and not to use the telephone.

Shortly after the mayor arrived, Chief Hummer contacted him by radio. It was decided that Governor Avery, Chief Hummer, and General Nickell should meet Wright, Jones, and Main at Civil Defense headquarters. They arrived within thirty minutes, and after brief discussion the group agreed to mobilize the National Guard, to set up police command posts, and to divide the stricken area into three sections: the southwest section was assigned to four hundred men from Forbes Air Force Base, the central section to the National Guard, and East Topeka to the Army Reserve. Chief Hummer would coordinate surveillance and control, and the police would patrol the entire area. Because the telephone installations had been badly damaged, Chief Hummer assigned one radio car to each command post for communication. Between 9:00 P.M. and 11:00 P.M. Wright and Hummer patrolled the city, surveying damage and confirming the boundaries of the stricken area, which had been tentatively identified by Civil Defense workers earlier. At 11:00 P.M., Wright had a conference with the city commissioners, the county commissioners, General Nickell, the commander from Forbes Air Force Base, Jones, and city and county department heads, to discuss problems of clean-up, resources available, and the mechanism for allocating resources to appropriate areas. As noted in Chapter 5, Harder arrived at 2:00 A.M. and volunteered to direct a thorough search-and-rescue operation. The operation was to start at daybreak and search for any injured or dead who might have been missed by the earlier, and necessarily hasty, police search.

THE MAKING OF THE EPHEMERAL GOVERNMENT

Disaster thus precipitated among these officials the same immediate drive to action which characterized the citizens in general. But the city officials, unlike the mass of citizens, had obvious and relevant tasks to perform. The need for immediate coordination, which was painfully clear, led them to meet at once to make plans. From this coalition of individuals variously linked by formal and informal ties grew the functioning executive organization of the ephemeral government.

Throughout the disaster period the headquarters of Civil Defense served as the focal point for the ephemeral government. Here were the necessary supplies, the maps, the radio center, and the portable transceivers. For the first few days, it was the center of all activity.

Although the degree of effective coordination was impressive, not everything ran well. The Civil Defense organization, operating for the first time in a realistic emergency situation, encountered unanticipated demands for which it was not prepared. Thus, its radio system was not completely compatible with that of city agencies. For several days Mayor Wright did not know about the hot line to the police department; and Civil Defense had no step-by-step emergency plan for disaster. Despite these difficulties, the presence of the Civil Defense headquarters with its equipment proved to be enormously helpful to the ephemeral government.

Leadership of the synthetic organization was assumed by Mayor Wright. He made appointments and directed the meetings. The fit between personality and role was a good one. One man, influential in the synthetic organization, said,

I have known [the mayor] for years, and he's really made for this type of situation. His whole personality is geared for this type of thing. It's when it's settled down that he lets the things that he says begin to hurt him; for he has the tendency, I think, to speak sometimes without thinking. But golly, at a time like this, you couldn't ask for a better man. He *knows* everybody. He knows them by *name*. He knows what *groups* to get, who can take care of this, and organize that, and he *knows* every facet of the community. And he set up some real good appointments and committees. He really moved well.

The mayor's mode of operation was basically autocratic, although his style allowed people to volunteer for tasks and for him to make assignments through requests rather than direction. He was personalistic, and by utilizing informal social networks developed through his political activities, and by using the power and resources available as mayor, he received unexcelled support. At his level, as at all lower levels, people were not inclined to question orders or plans. Governmental bureaucracy too was changed by the mood of the post-disaster Utopia, and red tape virtually disappeared.

THE OUTSIDE CORNUCOPIA

In the tangled aftermath of the storm came an acute need for manpower and equipment to clear the debris. The city and county mobilized all available equipment, and private contractors volunteered more. Manpower and machines came from Kansas City, Missouri, and from such cities in Kansas as Clifton, Emmett, Hiawatha, Holton, Junction City, Kansas City, Lawrence, Leavenworth, Leawood, Mission, Mulvane, Olathe, Ottawa, Overland Park, Salina, and Wichita. Men and equipment were known to have been sent to Topeka from Jackson County, Missouri, and from the following Kansas counties: Brown, Douglas, Franklin, Jefferson, Johnson, Leavenworth, Lyon, Nemaha, Osage, Saline, Sedgwick, and Wyandotte. Private contractors from as far away as Memphis, Tennessee, sent help; and individuals who owned trucks, tractors, chain saws, and other power tools converged on Topeka to offer assistance. All these resources were coordinated by Richard Hanger, a county commissioner, from his headquarters in the county garage.

The restoration of semipublic property—gas, water, power, and telephone—was the responsibility of the utility involved. Damage to power and telephone facilities was extensive. Each utility sent repairmen into the stricken city within thirty minutes; before daylight, crews and equipment were working, and men and equipment were moving toward Topeka from other communities. Ten days later, the task of restoring all utilities had been completed.

In a sense, the utility companies worked independently of the ephemeral government. Trained crews, proper equipment, and supervisory personnel already existed, ready to be thrown into the breach. However, their work had to be coordinated with the governing group, since repair of utilities was a vital part of the restoration of the affected area.

The cornucopia not only poured forth men and equipment; aid in planning and coordination came as well. Within forty-eight hours, experts from the Office of Emergency Planning were in Topeka. Personnel from the Urban Renewal Agency and Forbes' Photo Reconnaissance worked together to examine aerial photographs of the area and provide preliminary estimates of the extent of damage. The Corps of Engineers sent in teams to survey the area; by Saturday noon the extent of damage was certified. President Johnson declared Topeka a disaster area, which automatically made available a million dollars for assistance in restoring public facilities.

The ephemeral government also incorporated within itself two outside organizations—the Red Cross, directed by Burnell Southall, and the volunteer organization, directed by Dr. Harder. The Red Cross worked with the ephemeral government in a coordinated, but semi-independent way. Immediately after the tornado, the Red Cross effected its standardized procedures for setting up mass feeding, providing shelter, and securing food, clothing and hand tools for the victims' relief. As we have noted earlier, these emergency centers took on a separate life of their own during the immediate crisis period. With its historic connection to medicine, the Red Cross distributed emergency medical supplies and service. Its activated its nationwide network of disaster workers: within forty-eight hours a complete organization was established in Topeka.

Red Cross officials estimated that approximately one hundred thousand meals were served from June 8 through June 20. Seven shelters were established. As it turned out, these shelters were used mostly by volunteer workers from other cities, rather than by storm victims. The shelters provided housing, offered a nurse and emergency medical aid, and provided long-term medical aid for the injured. The Red Cross also established six points through which tons of clothing were distributed. In sum, 1,530 applications were processed by the Red Cross, and slightly less than half a million dollars distributed. Red Cross rehabilitation grant applications were completed by 688 people. Rehabilitation help was also made available from personal savings, insurance, loans, and other sources.

The indigenous volunteer organization, which was directly responsible to the mayor, has been described in Chapter 5. This organization coordinated city, county, Red Cross, Salvation Army, and individual contributions of goods and time.

These resources were supplemented by the Job Corps, which sent two hundred young men into the area from four camps in the Middle West. The job corpsmen were housed twenty miles away, at the University of Kansas, and were transported to and from the area. Arriving in Topeka on June 12, 150 of them remained for ten days, while an additional 50 from the camp at Poplar Bluff, Missouri, stayed for three weeks. Job Corpsmen played a unique role, for among the nonvolunteer workers they alone *could* help clear up private property, which the city and county crews were forbidden to touch. Although directed by a Job Corps foreman, these men were under the control of the local volunteer organization. The remaining clean-up of public property was managed by the Corps of Engineers, with payment provided from emergency funds from the Office of Emergency Planning. Little controversy marked this effort. The need was obvious, and the task clear-cut. The only public question was raised by some residents of East Topeka, who complained that clean-up crews had given inadequate attention to their section of town.

As with any new organization, the ephemeral government did not operate at 100 percent efficiency. Sometimes trucks and high-loaders used to cart debris appeared at one place while the crew arrived at another; sometimes difficulty arose when equipment and personnel were moved; several volunteer crews simply disappeared. The available equipment was not always appropriate to the task; there was, for instance, much acrimonious comment on the inefficiencies of radio communication. Yet, given the nature of the challenge, the coping capacity of the ephemeral government was impressive; it met the basic adaptive needs of the urban system and moved toward a rational organization of effort in the face of chaos. It provided a reasonable division of labor, in that tasks were appropriately defined and job assignments made. It secured resources and methods of allocation. By its provision of an executive power structure, community-wide decisions were made and implemented. And finally, it provided a system of communication which made possible a coordination and integration of effort.

The accomplishments and limitations of the ephemeral government stand out most vividly when its work is compared with the functioning of the utility companies. The crews from the utility company were trained for their jobs, had often worked together on similar tasks, had access to familiar and appropriate equipment, and had developed routine procedures for centralized control. No shift in their roles was needed, for to them the tornado represented an event differing in quantity, but not quality, from normal experiences.

In contrast, the challenge that faced the ephemeral government was more difficult. It not only had the task of clearing public property—a task analogous to that of the utility company—but was also responsible for the health and safety of the entire population. It had to integrate various public and private agencies over which it had no formal control. The Red Cross, for example, was not subordinate to the mayor; it acted in a coordinated but independent manner. Even the local Civil Defense group was not responsible to the mayor. In this sense, the community depended, as the utility company did not, on the willingness of the various components of the synthetic organization to cooperate. In Topeka, such cooperation and voluntary subordination was extended virtually without exception. We see here another example of the utopian mood writ large.

THE DYNAMICS OF THE EPHEMERAL GOVERNMENT

In introducing this chapter, we asked how it was that disaster could precipitate a radical yet functional reorganization of the city's government, a sudden transmutation of social forms which, in the ordinary course of events, seem notably resistant to change. The answer seems to lie in the revised basis for social order which arose from the counter-disaster syndrome, and the varied phenomena of the post-disaster Utopia. Faced with ambiguity, and with tasks of overwhelming magnitude, the latent resources of informal association were utilized to the full. In the charged and personalistic atmosphere of the post-disaster period, the usual issues of territoriality and formal rights were laid aside, and new organizational forms and roles developed with startling rapidity. This was true of the ephemeral volunteer crews and the ephemeral organizations; it was true too of the ephemeral government. In a sense, there seemed no choice. Either those responsible for the city's weal rose to the challenge or the city perished.

There is perhaps a lesson here for civil planning. Theoretically, a Civil Defense organization should be prepared to coordinate community efforts in time of disaster, but the system and the bureaucratic roles of its officials seem inadequate in dealing with an actual emergency. The Civil Defense organization is an attempt to rationalize disaster and to reduce it to plans and principles; its smooth bureaucratic operation depends upon a stable and predictable environment. Rapid change, policy shifts, compromise, and improvisation are foreign to a bureaucratic operation. Yet these are the responses demanded by disaster. And these are the responses that a good politician, through his knowledge of the informal social structure of the community, is trained to make. It was understandable that the mayor could say, "We had no plan," while the Civil Defense director pointed to the "payoff" of Civil Defense planning. It was understandable that when the mayor asked for a course of action to follow, he was given a 250-page book analyzing disaster rather than a condensed point-by-point checklist.

The Civil Defense organization did play a useful role. Its headquarters provided an adequate meeting place and an adequate communication system. But more generally, the civic strength, the roots of adequate adaptation, lay in the availability of relevant social resources, the existence of informal social networks which allowed quick coordination, and the social-psychological processes which for a time shifted the motivational and group structures of the city.

CHAPTER SEVEN

THE DISASTER RESPONSE
AND COLLECTIVE BEHAVIOR

W E HAVE SEEN how the disaster led to profound changes within the city, producing new forms of individual and social behavior. The changes were complex and interactive; individual reactions cumulated and led to new social responses; the social events in turn led to an ephemeral reorganization of the city's institutions and polity. In the preceding chapters we have attempted to unravel this complex skein of causality, to disentangle the convoluted network of events so as to arrive at a generalized view of the dynamics of disaster. In this chapter we shall move a step beyond phenomenological description. It is our purpose here to sketch out a more general view of the disaster process, and to show how an understanding of disaster can clarify other kinds of social change. We shall thus view the disaster which struck Topeka on June 8, 1966, not as a single crisis calling forth a unique set of adaptations, but rather as a particular case which sheds light on the more general processes of social adaptation. We shall begin by reviewing the processes detailed in the earlier chapters.

WHAT HAPPENS IN DISASTER

First there was the disaster, a precipitate physical disruption of the ordinary and expectable flow of life. It was the stimulus for all that followed.

Second, the physical disruption posed adaptive demands to individuals, groups, and institutions. At the individual level the demands were different for victims and nonvictims. The victims were faced with the tasks of survival in a situation of perceptual and cognitive deprivation. Threat and fear, which were omnipresent, had to be pushed aside in the interest of escape and family concern. The nonvictims too found their cues for action disrupted, yet, for many, action was a necessity. These varied individual demands, these tasks, produced different responses, some of which we have detailed in earlier chapters: the zombie-like "disaster syndrome" among the victims; the "counter-disaster" syndrome among the nonvictims; mass convergence, buzzing exchanges of information, and close monitoring of television and radio reports, as a response to the pressing need to "make sense" of the changed social world; and the occasional noninvolvement which seemed linked to characterological narcissism.

From these various demands and reactions arose the third major phenomenon: the development of that collective perspective which Wolfenstein (1957, p. 189) has called the "post-

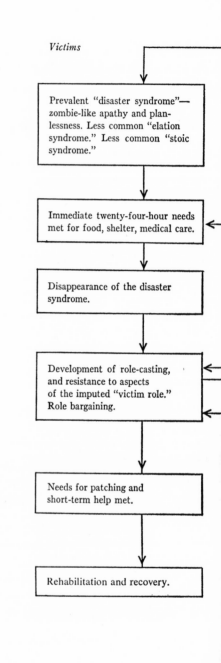

Victims

Prevalent "disaster syndrome"—
zombie-like apathy and plan-
lessness. Less common "elation
syndrome." Less common "stoic
syndrome."

Immediate twenty-four-hour needs
met for food, shelter, medical care.

Disappearance of the disaster
syndrome.

Development of role-casting,
and resistance to aspects
of the imputed "victim role."
Role bargaining.

Needs for patching and
short-term help met.

Rehabilitation and recovery.

FIGURE 1

THE SOCIAL AND INDIVIDUAL PHENOMENA OF DISASTER

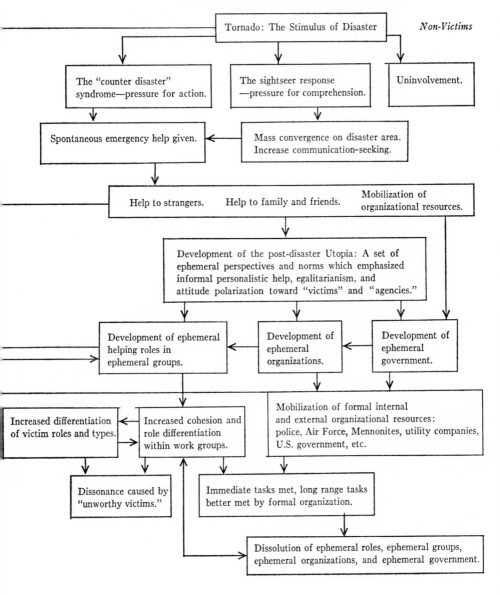

disaster Utopia." During the "utopian" period there quickly developed an ephemeral set of attitudes and norms, which for a while governed the relationships between people. The giving of help was valued, interactions were personalistic, barriers of class and color were partly disregarded, and a sense of shared fate was common. The utopian mood had its hostile obverse side—bureaucratic formalities and routinized procedures aroused great anger. In an ephemeral hagiography, the tornado victims became saints, and formal agencies became sinners.

The development and consolidation of this utopian perspective played a part in the fourth stage, the mobilization of organized social action in the service of recovery. We have detailed the emergence of an ephemeral government, ephemeral institutions, and ephemeral groups. For a brief period the city's organizational structures took on a new pattern, based in part on prior links of informal association, and in part upon new group formations. Pre-existing agencies were utilized, but often in new ways and for new tasks. In an astonishingly brief period new patterns of integration and coordination developed, and the demands for short-term help were met.

A fifth stage is discernible too: the stage of termination. We have shown how the ephemeral groups set in motion events which led to their own dissolution. They met the major short-term needs, and when this became apparent, the impetus for group action dissolved. Another, less-obvious process also played its part: the group action led to a clearer perception of the complexities of human reaction and the occasional cussedness of human nature, and against these harsh realities the tenuous perspectives of the post-disaster utopia were too feeble to survive.

We have pointed out how similar phenomena are reported from a variety of disasters. Figure 1 diagrams the linkage between these matters in greater detail. It shows *what* happened; it does not show why. But its phenomenological tracery will serve as an introduction to the issues raised by the more general study of collective behavior.

WHAT HAPPENS IN COLLECTIVE BEHAVIOR

Collective behavior is that branch of sociology which studies the emergence and development of *new and unexpected patterns of social action*. Riots, crazes, cults, panics, social movements— these are the phenomena of collective behavior. All are discontinuous phenomena, unexpected and out of the ordinary run of events.

Such discontinuous behavior should be clearly distinguished from the normal processes of society. Social change is usually evolutionary and flowing. Thus a pastor may adopt new behavior as his church becomes more liberal, or a contemporary father may find himself without much influence over his adolescent children; but these changes simply modify roles already in existence. In most social change the new social roles and positions and structures do not emerge *de novo*. They are not, so to speak, "invented"; they are not discontinuous.

The case is otherwise with collective behavior. People who participate in a riot, a craze, or a sect take on new patterns of social action. They are inventing new role behaviors for themselves, new social positions. This does not mean that everything within the collective behavior is entirely new. The rioter has shouted and run before; the cultist has attended other meetings and uttered other prayers. But in the total social context, the patterning of the behavior is new, and what the cultist or rioter does represents a discontinuity with the past.

Such collective behaviors emerge in a sequential series of stages, and their final forms are determined by what happens along the way. We may distinguish five stages in the emergence and development of collective behavior: (1) an initial social or physical change which leads to (2) social strains, collective unease, or discontent; this in turn results in (3) the development of perspectives as guides to new action; and from these comes (4) mobilization for action, along with (5) feedback of action into the social system. We shall briefly outline these five stages here, and then turn to a more specific consideration of each in turn.[1]

Social Change as Stimulus. Emergence of collective behavior, no matter what its form, is always linked to larger social change. Thus the United States riots of 1967 were linked to the changing role of the Negro in American society. The Nazi party arose from a Germany ruined by defeat, inflation, depression, and internal dissensus. Communist activity increases as a function of social discontent. The current student unrest is related to the dislocations of the Vietnamese War and the changing structure and function of the university. The stimulus for collective behavior is always some form of social change.

The Reaction of Strain. Not all changes lead to collective behavior, however. A change must not only occur, but it must pose some kind of adaptive demand; in terms of our earlier discussion (Chapter 2), it must pose adaptive *tasks*. Before collective behavior can occur there must be a sense of unrest, discontent, anguish, excitement. It is customary in sociology and in psychiatry to speak of *strain* resulting from change: we may equate the notion of strain with the notion of adaptive task. Different groups in society confront different adaptive tasks. In studying collective behavior we therefore must analyze not only the general changes in society, but also the adaptive tasks which these changes impose for particular groups.

The Development of Perspectives. Strains typically lead to a third process, here labeled as "the development of perspec-

---

[1] This particular typology of sequential stages is only one way of viewing the phenomenon: it corresponds most closely with the six conditions that Smelser (1962, pp. 15–18), holds to determine collective behavior: namely, structural conduciveness, structural strain, growth and spread of a generalized belief, precipitating factors, mobilization of participants for action, and operation of social control. Smelser's notion of "structural strain" here finds expression in the concept of strain as a shared adaptive task for individuals and organizations; "generalized belief" corresponds in part to our notion of "perspectives"; and "mobilization for action" is identical. The other elements of his typology refer to factors in the social field which allow communication and determine perceived options.

Sometimes people held informal parties atop the rubble. (*Photo courtesy of* Topeka Capital-Journal)

"*Mostly people just stood and looked at our trees, and made lots of comments about our gorgeous trees that weren't there any more.*" (*Photo courtesy of* Topeka Capital-Journal)

"It became impossible to absorb. You see all these trees down, and buildings down, and you can't absorb it or talk about it." (Photo courtesy of Topeka Capital-Journal)

"After we came out I had a feeling of disbelief, like a bad dream." (Red Cross photo by Palmer)

tives."[2] This is a high-flown way to refer to a very general phenomenon—the need for understanding, comprehension, and planning when confronted by adaptive demands. In the early stages of collective behavior rumors spread with remarkable ease. Man is an information-processing animal: confronted by strain—by new tasks—he needs to "make sense" of the situation, to develop an over-all map of the world which confronts him, and plan concrete action. The perspectives he develops may be simple, may be no more than shared moods or slogans—"Lynch the bastards," "The dam has broken!" "Flower power," "The only good Jap is a dead Jap." At the other extreme are the complex "ideologies," which give a coherent perspective of the world and its workings.

Stated in such cold terms, the development of simple perspectives or complex ideologies sounds a dry and logical matter, but dry and logical it is not. People respond to strain with affect as well as with intelligence, and the perspectives which they develop will include their feelings and moods, as well as their logic. During the early stages of collective behavior people often share a sense of excitement, kinship, exaltation; they develop highly polarized feelings—the saints versus the ungodly. Such feelings are given a justification and rationale by the emergent perspectives. Thus every religion has its ideology, but no one who has attended a revival meeting would regard this ideology as dry and abstruse. Nor would a participant in the Nuremberg rallies during the early stages of Nazism see this ideological movement as unemotional.

The Mobilization for Action. The new perspective—with its intermingled rationality and emotionality—generally leads

[2] Our usage here is in accord with that suggested by Becker, Geer, Hughes, and Strauss (1961, pp. 33, 34): "We use the term perspective to refer to a co-ordinated set of ideas and actions a person uses in dealing with some problematic situation, to refer to a person's ordinary way of thinking and feeling about and acting in such a situation." Group perspectives exist, as well as individual perspectives; the former are "perspectives held collectively by a group of people." Becker *et al.* (*ibid.*, pp. 33–37) provides a useful discussion of the notion's implications and limitations.

to action. A perspective is a cognitive map, and a map is useful only because it tells the traveler where to go and how to get there. Perspectives and ideologies are precursors to the act.

Collective action may take many forms. The simplest is of course the panic in which a crowd of unrelated individuals engages en masse in flight or fight behavior. At the other extreme is the social movement, with its organized groups of the faithful, its planned programs of action, its deliberate strategies, tactics, and goals. Action may thus occur without much social organization, or it may give rise to very complex organizational structures. Not only does the degree of complexity differ, but also the *kind* of action will vary. The action may be direct, aimed at achieving new social benefits or resisting social change; or at the other extreme it may attempt to change the nature of man or to prepare the world for some anticipated millennium—the latter being indirect responses to the social challenge. The action may focus on a few specific issues, or it may have an exceedingly diffuse focus. The acting group may take a highly protesting stance and call for radical action, or, at the other extreme, it may be highly accommodating and evolutionary. Collective behavior may be transient or long-lived; if it is long-lived, it will exhibit much change. The sect militant may be replaced by the church smug; the Bolshevik revolutionary by the bureaucratic commissar. Thus in analyzing collective behavior we need to look also at the time dimension and the historical processes of growth and change.

Feedback with Secondary Strain. Once action is under way, it develops a dynamic of its own. Collective action aims at change; its goal is the reduction of strain. But change in turn affects the collective response. Thus we may speak of a fifth stage, the stage of feedback. Action leads to change, which leads often to new action. Sometimes the feedback may be unexpected: the collective behavior may produce *secondary strains* which in turn lead to new perspectives. A particularly interesting kind of feedback occurs when the collective behavior takes organizational form, for the mere fact of social organization sets certain processes in motion, and creates certain unexpected strains. Factions arise, charismatic qualities are imputed to leaders—and then taken away again—and the organization itself begins to make managerial demands. The results of all this are often surprising to the participants. Many of those who followed Fidel Castro into the Sierra Maestra found themselves caught up in a far more radical revolution than they had ever anticipated. The majority of the founders of the American Constitution had no real desire, in the beginning, to sever ties with England. Action has a way of producing consequences outside the original anticipations, and so forcing new adaptations.

DISASTER AS A STIMULUS TO COLLECTIVE BEHAVIOR

Phenomenologically, it is clear that the disaster response is one particular species of collective behavior. It is a discontinuous form of social change; it is precipitated by an event which poses new adaptive tasks and strains; it gives rise to a set of perspectives—the post-disaster Utopia—which serves as a guide to action; it leads to the development of new organizational forms; and it changes as a result of feedback with secondary strain. Along its ephemeral course it gives rise to intense commitments and polarizations; leadership arises, sometimes with charismatic overtones; factionalism develops; new roles and identifications emerge.

In these ways it is like other forms of collective behavior, yet it is also unique. Unlike most collective behavior, the disaster response is precipitated by a clear and obvious change. The adaptive tasks are basically the same after every community-wide disaster; and the collective responses are essentially similar, at least in similar communities. Disaster thus provides a kind of simplified and repeatable natural experiment, an experiment which allows us to examine the dynamics of collective behavior in "pure culture." The disaster response differs from the other forms of collective behavior in which the precipitating social changes are unclear, unrepeatable, and ambiguous, and in which the collective processes themselves are complex, interactive, and often obscure. By studying the dynamics of the disaster response, we may be able to clarify the processes which are inexplicable and hidden in other forms of collective behavior.

In the preceding chapters we have discussed the reaction of a single city to a single event. We have shown that similar reactions have been observed in other cities after other disasters. We have attempted to clarify the ways in which individual reactions led to group action, and how the pre-existing social structures of the city—formal and informal—provided the framework for newly emergent behavior. We have assumed that similar dynamics underlie the similar phenomena reported in other studies. This, be it noted, is an *assumption,* and not tested here by any comparative data. We will now extend this assumption beyond disaster. We will examine certain phenomena often observed in other types of collective behavior, and see whether our view of disaster dynamics can shed light on these more widespread and general phenomena. This is not to claim that the disaster response, as one particular form of collective behavior, can be generalized so as to explain completely *all* collective behavior. We suggest, however, that insight derived from one form of collective behavior can illuminate other forms.

We shall begin by suggesting a few ways in which the strains of disaster are similar to the strains which precipitate other forms of collective behavior. These strains lead to a quest for perspectives and to the utopian mood. We shall suggest that something similar to the utopian mood is often found during the early stages in other types of collective behavior. Polarization of attitude is part of the utopian mood, and part too of most collective episodes; we suggest certain processes which underlie it. Not always do perspectives lead to group formation; we consider the circumstances necessary for collective organization to develop. Finally, we consider briefly the emergence of leadership and charisma, and the responses to secondary strain. To all of these general issues we apply insights developed from studying the particular responses to Topeka's unique disaster.[3]

THE TASKS OF CHANGE

In our earlier chapters we have discussed the social and personality demands imposed by the tornado; as we shall see, these demands are not limited to the disaster situation. For the victim in its path, the disaster posed an immediate task: he had to deal with a radically disrupted environment. He also faced the task of warding off intense and disruptive feelings: for the sake of his own and his family's survival he could not allow himself to give way to panic or anguish. The arrival of help brought new task demands. The victim for the first time faced the task of seeing himself as someone in need of help. For many, this raised the spectre of dependency—how could a reasonably independent person, priding himself on his own resourcefulness and abilities, accept what seemed like charity? The helpers also forced the victim to mobilize his energies in the service of future planning, and forced the would-be helpers to define the options and limits of effective action.

Outside the tornado area, the citizens faced other tasks. For

[3] Although not a dominant theme in the disaster literature, the similarities between disaster response and other forms of collective behavior have been pointed out by several authors. Thus Fritz (1961, p. 655), in summarizing the disaster literature, suggests that "disaster studies provide the social scientist with perhaps his best opportunity to develop generalizations about human nature and the basic processes of social interaction." His discussion is highly congruent with our observations of the Topeka experience. Shaskolsky (undated) too has melded observations of disaster response to larger societal theories, focusing especially upon volunteerism as a response to the *Gemeinschaft* nature of society after disaster. Dynes and Quarantelli (1968) have attempted to apply the perspectives of both organizational analysis and collective behavior analysis to disaster responses. Although the results are not completely in accord with our observations, the discussion is interesting in its own right. To the best of our knowledge, however, the present chapter is unique in attempting not to analyze disaster from an "outside" paradigm—be it a paradigm drawn from collective behavior or from organizational theory—but rather to treat the disaster response as one type of collective behavior, which can be analyzed in the same terms as a riot or a social movement.

those with family or friends in the stricken area, the pressing task was to provide emergency help. The nonvictim too had a significant portion of his landscape disrupted. What did the tornado mean for him? For Topeka? What did it feel like, what did it portend? At one remove, the nonvictim also needed to integrate the change into his larger plans and actions.

Beyond such immediate needs, the potential task posed by community survival confronted some, but not all, of the nonvictims. In general, those people who tended to hold an empathic identification with others took on this task; those who saw themselves as detached, alienated, or in some sense "outside" did not. Many people viewed the tornado as a threat to their own ability and sense of mastery, and thus were challenged to take direct and immediate action against it.

Another kind of task confronted that group of people who had organizational responsibility. For the police, the tornado posed an organizational task—that of providing social controls in the disrupted area. Other organizations too were confronted by major needs: communications were shattered, gas and water pipes were burst. Those responsible for such services faced a sudden and overwhelming task in reinstituting facilities. At a higher social level, the mayor and city commission needed to plan and think through the steps of tornado recovery, not for themselves but for the organizations of the community.

The physical changes produced by the tornado were specific to the disaster situation, but the tasks—individual, group, societal —which confronted the citizenry were not. Similar tasks tend to arise whenever any calamitous or large-scale change disrupts the social organism. Cantril (1941, p. 63), for instance, sees as a basis for all social movements "a chaotic external environment which he [the individual] cannot interpret. . . ." A more cogent description of the tornado's aftermath would be hard to find: for victims and nonvictims the expectable environment was chaotically disrupted. Blumer (1951, p. 200) views collective behavior as arising largely when "people have come to form new conceptions of themselves which do not conform to the actual positions which they occupy in their lives." We saw this in the abrupt transition of roles encountered by victim and helper alike. And Toch (1965, p. 11) has the most general formulation of all: "For a person to be led to join a social movement, he must not only sense a problem, but must also (1) feel that something can be done about it and (2) want to do something about it himself." Although useless as a definition for collective behavior alone—it would as easily describe what happens when a tire goes flat on the highway—it is relevant to the disaster response. In these ways at least, there is a formal correspondence between some aspects of disaster-induced strain and the kinds of strain which lead to collective behavior in general.

In yet another way the strains arising from tornado provide, in microscopic view, a picture of larger social process. Social strains often involve more than a single problem or single adaptive demand. Strains may involve a profound challenge to the sense of self. Erickson (1956, pp. 114–15) has spoken of this as a problem of "ego identity": he writes of the total challenge which sometimes occurs:

We may well pause to ponder briefly the over-all fact that the technological and economic developments of our day encroach upon all traditional group identities and solidarities such as may have developed in agrarian, feudal, patrician, or mercantile ideologies. As has been shown by many writers, such over-all development seems to result in a loss of sense of cosmic wholeness, of providential planfulness, and of heavenly sanction for the means of production (and destruction). In large parts of the world this seems to result in a ready fascination with totalistic world views, views predicting millenniums and cataclysms, and advocating self-appointed mortal gods.

In Topeka we saw something akin to this as a result of the disruption of the expectable environment: people felt at times "all at sea," a feeling which resulted in apathy and a loss of direction. A few psychologically sophisticated informants spoke of a felt loss of identity, as if the loss of the physical objects, the behavior settings to which they were accustomed and through which they moved, somehow produced a threat to the self.

Social change does not lead all individuals to collective action, even when it might seem appropriate. Necessary too is a feeling of identification, of shared fate, with a reference group. Karl Marx long ago pointed to "class consciousness" as a prerequisite to organizational activity among the proletariat. In Topeka too the acceptance of a volunteer organizational task was predicated on a larger sense of identity—in this case not with class or group, but with the city and the injured. The tasks of group action thus may pose similar issues for the disaster response and for other forms of collective behavior.

We also observed something in Topeka which has not been much discussed in the literature of collective behavior, yet has implications beyond this disaster and this city. Social change confronts the individual with adaptive demands, and *sometimes the individual can use pre-existing organizations to meet these demands*. When this happens the organization may take on new forms and functions, and may provide the matrix for new types of behavior. Thus the ephemeral organizations developed in the context of services provided by older formal organizations, and the ephemeral government gave new patterns and functions to pre-existing agencies. In other places too the organizational responses to change may play a major part in defining the tasks and options available to the collectivity. Not always will the task responses of the formal organizations fit as neatly with the task responses of the mass as was true after the tornado. But interaction there will be.

THE DEVELOPMENT OF PERSPECTIVES

Man is an adaptive animal. Confronted with unexpected tasks, his first impulse is toward action. Action cannot take place in a vacuum: if a task is to be met, the actor must assess the available options and priorities. So it is in disaster; people must make sense of this sudden new environment before they can take collective arms against it. Each individual sees only a small part of the total picture; each individual needs knowledge. In order to form his own cognitive map of the tasks and possibilities before him, he turns to others and seeks information any way he can. This information is assessed and shared through a complex interactive process. In times of general social strain rumors fly; the propensity for belief is high; people interact with surprising freedom and intensity. Sociologists commonly observe a "milling" of crowds prior to rioting or mob action; this milling may be regarded as a form of information exchange. Even the spread of rumor may be seen as an attempt to exchange information in the service of collective perspectives.

In a national crisis people remain glued to their radios or television sets and eagerly discuss every new tidbit of available information. The local crisis of the tornado had the same effect: it led most people to seek information, to share it, and to quest for a total picture of the destruction. The television and radio stations interrupted all programing to feed a constant stream of commentary, eye-witness reports, and interview material to the eager listeners. For several days after the tornado little routine work was done in office and factory; instead the workers used every available minute to talk about what had happened to them or to people they had known. This general milling and buzzing seems an invariant response to collective strain.

From such information—sought, shared, collectively interpreted, and assessed—comes a more complete understanding of the strain and its sources. But it is not understanding alone which is sought; the push is toward action. Therefore, understanding which gives rise to action is especially valued. We shall refer to this general push toward understanding plus action as "the building of perspectives." It is through the development of perspectives that the human being is able to discover strategies which seem appropriate to his collective needs.

When we speak of perspectives, we refer not only to the explanations—the beliefs—which people adopt, but also to the moods and sentiments that go with such beliefs, and the general plans and strategies for action which result. In our analysis of the disaster response, three kinds of perspectives stand out with special clarity. One we have labeled the "mood of the post-disaster Utopia." Another was the elementary social division and formation of social roles around the complimentary tasks of the victim and the helpers. A third, emerging from these two, was the inclination to divide the world into saints and sinners, with many nonvictims assigning to bureaucracy the role of the sinner and to the volunteers the role of saint. It should be pointed out that these kinds of perspectives were not unique to Topeka: they are reported from many other disaster sites, and similar phenomena are reported for other types of collective behavior. The following paragraphs work toward a general theory to explain the emergence of such specific perspectives as a response to social strain.

THE UTOPIAN MOOD: IDEOLOGY, TASK, AND REALITY

The Utopian Mood as Proto-ideology. We shall look first at the development of the "post-disaster Utopia" as a kind of perspective. We have described how, after disaster, formal rules and regulations were laid aside, the usual distinctions between rich and poor disregarded. For a time there was an almost palpable sense of community cohesion, and many people felt an unselfish concern for the welfare of others. Those who remembered World War II compared this period to the spirit of the London blitz. For a brief time, it seemed as if the golden rule might indeed serve as a guide to action.

Such a utopian mood is common to disasters, as reported by Wolfenstein (1957). It is not, however, unique to them; it has been reported for other times and places as well. Especially is it seen in the early phases of social movements, and among small sectarian associations. Wordsworth has told how the beginning of the French Revolution affected him: "France standing on the top of golden hours / And human nature seeming born again."

The Nazi party saw a similar utopian mood: the collective image of good Nazis was defined by one as "men who left their wives, families and parents, preferring the sacred sign of the swastika to their means of livelihood!" (Abel, 1965, pp. 145–46). Small sects, like that of Father Divine (Cantril, 1941) or the Diggers and early Quakers (Cohn, 1957) were notable for their sense of communal involvement, their sense of fellowship, kinship, and neighborliness. A similar spirit has occasionally been noted for the contemporary youth movement, the Woodstock Festival of 1969 being a well-publicized example. The utopian mood is a concomitant of the kind of communal order which Ferdinand Toennies has described as *gemeinschaft*—a society based on shared sentiments rather than legalistic exchange and rational calculation. It is precisely this kind of communal order which (in less extreme and dramatic form) also seems to underlie much informal organization.

Since the utopian mood has collective consequences, its sources need clarification. What are the conditions which lead to its development? to its decline? What are its limits? And how can it be understood within the general theory of collective behavior? The experience of Topeka may provide a fruitful source of understanding.

Tasks and the Utopian Mood. The building of perspectives starts with an attempt to gather information, to develop a new mapping of probabilities, options, and priorities. Novel ways of meeting the tasks become clear. As these are discussed and defined, a consensus develops. In the development of this consensus a strong motivating force is provided by the poignant feeling of empathic involvement, the need to master and cope, the occasional uneasy sense of guilt. Without such strong motivation it is doubtful that the usual concerns of role and status could have been held in temporary abeyance. The group task of tornado recovery had high priority, in part because it provided a means for accomplishing pressing individual tasks as well. It was good to offer temporary shelter to victims. It was good to donate materials to meet emergency needs. It was good to volunteer food or help. It was good to set aside the formalities of the credit bureau when the needs were immediate and future payment seemed reasonably assured. Consensus was largely achieved.

The development of group consensus made possible the emergence of new forms of coordinated action and reciprocal expectation, even when individuals acted for themselves and not as members of an organized group. The Volunteer Center did not have to worry much about procuring food; food simply appeared, donated by individuals and by storeowners. Bedding, clothing, and material appeared as if from a cornucopia. The few cases in which the donor departed from the emergency norms and tried to set limits to his charity (one man tried to donate new suits, and asked that they be given only to people who were in the business world) were greeted with annoyance and antagonism. In short, the group norms developed from the collective processes of task definition; they provided cues to individual task-oriented action; and they set limits on acceptable behavior.

The fact that the total community shared a general task of high priority led also to a great sense of cohesion and community pride. It is a truism in sociology that group cohesion increases as people work cooperatively and successfully on a shared task. This is valid for small experimental groups observed in the laboratory (Deutsch, 1949; Thomas, 1957), for military units (Janowitz and Little, 1965), for youngsters in summer camp (Sherif et al., 1954), and for interracial contact (Davis, 1957). High school coaches use this principle when they try to instill a "team spirit"; personnel managers employ it when they try to involve the workers as participants in the over-all goals of the factory. For a time in Topeka the bulk of the citizens saw themselves as cooperatively involved in a common task, and the result was a great sense of community cohesion. People felt close, neighborly; the barriers to interpersonal communication were markedly reduced.

In Topeka the utopian mood grew from the perception that

common tasks were shared by the entire community. The same dynamics explain other situations in which the utopian mood is found—the early development of nationalistic fervor, commitment to total war, initial stages of revolution, and sectarian social movements. Such situations usually are found at times of intense social stress, of economic insecurity, of physical attack, of precipitous social change, of despair with the present, and of status decline. The utopian mood develops if and only if the community or group feels it has "found an answer" to its problems— that is, that it has arrived at a group consensus. This consensus is essentially a consensus on the general *task* confronting the group. If the task is perceived as being transcendentally important, and if it is widely shared, and if initial consensus on the means or norms of task acomplishment is present, the utopian mood appears. This step-wise process may be diagrammed as follows for the general case:

shared common tasks of high priority + communication and perception of the shared nature of the task + shared agreement on reciprocal individual behavior appropriate to task accomplishment

| (leads to)

1. A sense of shared closeness with others involved in accomplishing task—i.e., the group or community.

2. Enhanced group cohesion, sentiments of warmth and concern.

3. Emergence of novel personalistic patterns of interaction with others.

+

Continued on page 160

4. Relative disregard
of status distinctions.

+

5. Relative disregard
of status norms governing
transactions between groups

=

↓

THE UTOPIAN MOOD

Utopia and Reality. The utopian mood is transient, and in Topeka its disappearance caused some sense of loss. "The tornado brought out the best in people," we were told; and regrets were voiced that "people couldn't be like that all the time." The foregoing analysis makes clear why the post-disaster Utopia was necessarily transient, since change in any step of development would lead to change in the final outcome. The priority of the shared tasks may lessen; or people may come to perceive that the task is not so shared as they had thought; or disagreement about the kind of individual behavior appropriate to task accomplishment may arise. All of these shifts could be observed within a few days after the tornado. The demand for immediate and flexible help was met in the main, and help-giving itself was increasingly routinized and handled by specialists. People no longer had pressing and immediate needs which called for immediate action. The dangerous trees had been cut down; roofs had been patched temporarily with plastic. The long-term tasks of recovery required a specialized bureaucracy with specialized roles and rationalized procedures—insurance adjusters, claim investigators, street crews, and so forth. The decreased priority of the shared collective task signaled the disappearance of the post-disaster Utopia.

But even before this the utopian mood was shifting. We have noted the strains that the "unworthy victim" imposed upon Mrs. Brown when she first began her volunteer role: the "unworthy victim" gave dramatic evidence that the task was not communally shared. For some volunteers this meant a retreat away from the

personalistic encounter, and toward a more universalistic orientation to the specialized job. Chapter 4 has detailed this development in a single work crew. A similar confrontation occurred
when a small group of citizens in the low-income area of town
held a protest meeting, claiming discrimination. Such protest,
widely perceived as unwarranted, struck at the roots of the
utopian mood.

Equally disruptive to the utopian mood is the emergence of
factionalism among different groups, and disagreement on the
kinds of behavior most appropriate to recovery. This was not a
major problem in Topeka, although its seeds were present in the
conflict between the volunteers and the Red Cross, a conflict described in the case of Mrs. Brown, and explored more fully in
Chapter 5. Factionalism was not disruptive because the utopian
mood had already dissipated before factionalism became organized. Yet in other circumstances factionalistic disagreement may
be the major cause for the dissolution of the utopian spirit. Any
successful revolution immediately enters a second stage of struggle
between extremists and moderates; the factionalism of religious
sects is commonplace; and even in warfare factional disagreement
may lead to internal disunion. Confronted with such stress, the
utopian mood is far too fragile to survive. The individual becomes
once again the private citizen, concerned less with the collective
need than with the cultivation of his own garden.

The utopian mood thus is self-limiting. It results from shared
beliefs in the nature of the problem and in the strategies for over-
coming it. It also gives rise to precise definitions of specific types
of action. The focus on action produces a new reality and poses
new problems. Unforeseen personal and group strains emerge. The
perspectives then change, and the utopian mood fades away. Thus
the utopian perspective should be seen not as cause or consequence
alone, but as one stage in a continuing feedback process whereby
the average citizen is able to adapt to crisis. A similar process of
emergence and decay seems to occur in the early stages of development of many types of collective behavior. If the social stresses

have resulted in the shared definition of common and reciprocal tasks, the utopian mood emerges. The mood then promotes a period of enthusiasm and high morale, which inevitably fades as priorities shift, or as different strategies of task accomplishment vie for adherence.

While the utopian mood remains, it may have the most profound social consequences. Close-knit and communal groups have the potential for producing major changes in a collective identity. Margaret Mead (1956) has described how a small sectarian movement among the Melanesians led to an almost total change of life style and patterns of social behavior. In the same way, many a small Protestant sect provides a comforting home for the rural newcomer to the big city, a home in which he can make the transition to the urban environment. The utopian mood does not always fade immediately, nor do its effects always disappear.

In-group, Out-group, and Collective Polarization. For every heaven there has to be a hell, for every saint a devil, and for every utopia a scapegoat. In Topeka, as in many other disasters, a scapegoat was provided by the formal functioning of bureaucracy, especially as perceived in the Red Cross. We have earlier considered in detail the sources of this disaffection, and there seems little need to repeat the analysis here. On the other hand, the process has more general implications which seem worthy of explication.

The utopian mood emerged among people who were suddenly faced with tasks of overwhelming priority; this is another way of saying that they were under excessive strain and highly motivated. For the most part no immediate channels existed for meeting the tasks at hand, and as a result they invented their roles and procedures for themselves. There was a certain zest to this process, the excitement of pioneering. Out of this high motivation, out of the zest, and out of all the new behaviors emerged the utopia. This process was not shared by all. There were some people in Topeka whose duties were clearly relevant to disaster, and who had only to turn to their usual procedures to find the forms which seemed appropriate to the task at hand. For them there was no need to develop radical new perspectives: it was enough if they could adapt the perspectives already available. Especially was this the case with those organizations officially involved with disaster: the Red Cross, the police, the utility company crews, and the Civil Defense.

However, two things happened which were somewhat unexpected. First, these agencies could not always respond in a sufficiently flexible manner. Second, the bureaucratic safeguards which were built into their procedures seemed exactly contrary to the values implicit in the post-disaster Utopia. The average helper in the Volunteer Center saw no virtue in filling out forms or going through a lengthy interview; his immediate response was to accept all victims at face value and give, within feasible limits, the aid they requested. He was impatient with waiting lines, angry at any lack of empathic involvement. Immediate help was good; anything which stood in the way was bad. Perhaps under more normal circumstances he would have felt only a mild but philosophical impatience with bureaucracy, but here his involvement was high and motivation intense. Bureaucratic delay in this situation produced a sense of anger verging on rage. Such anger, it should be noted, was much more extreme among the volunteers than among the victims themselves: the latter seemed more than willing to wait their turn and take their bureaucratic chances.

These observations may have bearing on the general process by which collective behavior develops its scapegoats. Generally, people involved in an episode of collective action are intensely motivated, and are led by this very intensity to place high value upon their perspectives. But not everybody around them is motivated by the same pressures, nor committed to the same tasks. If one kind of perspective provides a definition of the good and the true, then those who fail to accord are by definition neither good nor true, they are false and unworthy. People outside the sphere of the angels can only be devils. It is perhaps this process which lends special virulence to the bitter factional quarrels after revolution—a stage which has been described by Brinton (1952) as "the reign of terror and virtue." The dynamics which emerge with such bloody clarity as we observe a Robespierre, a Marat, a Stalin, or a Red Guard, may have their mild analogue in the reaction of Topekans to differences in disaster perspectives.

Role Taking, Role Giving, and Collective Disillusion. The moods described above emerged from the tasks confronting the stricken city. But a perspective is more than a mood, it is also a system of perceptions, understandings, and beliefs. It is a way of organizing and conceptualizing the world. It thus has its cognitive as well as its emotive aspects. In Topeka, it seems easiest to describe these cognitive portions of the perspectives in terms of role assignment and role taking.

The most obvious of the role divisions in Topeka was that between victim and helper. This would seem to be a simple enough discrimination, but in practice it was not always so simple. We have seen in earlier chapters how not all of the citizens took on the role of helper, and how not all of the victims easily accepted the implications of their new status. In fact, the average victim often took a while to decide that the label fit him as it did the person next door. Perhaps this reluctance was reasonable, and not simply because of the implication of dependency. People caught in the path of the tornado had many needs, some of which were seen by the helpers and some of which were not. The helpers tended to impute certain needs to victims. Most often the imputation was correct, but not always. Between individual victims and helpers there frequently ensued a bargaining process; the victim did not totally accept the definition thrust upon him by the helper, but rather tried to establish his own tasks and needs as relevant to the helper's perception. The net result of this process was a lessening of volunteer enthusiasm and a partial reformulation of the helper's role.

Would it be straining too much to suggest an analogy here between disaster and those kinds of social movements which seek to impute or give a role to a particular class of people? Collective movements often work toward the conversion of certain groups: the Communist party proselytizes among the working class, the the Temperance League among the drinking class, and the sectarian religions among the godless sinners. There is often a discordance between the way the faithful view their potential converts and the way the potential converts view themselves. The American workingman may not feel exploited, the casual drinker may not see himself as on the road to ruination, and the man who can take church or leave it alone may still view himself as a good Christian. This discordance can be most discouraging to those involved in the social movement. In fact, most American Communists have tended to avoid direct proselytizing whenever possible (Krugman, 1952); the temperance leagues tend more to mobilize the faithful than to convert the drinker (Gusfield, 1954); and lay members of religious groups need a special kind of organizational control in order to engage in missionary activities. What was a minor process in Topeka may have major repercussions for the extended social movement.

Ambiguity, Perspectives, and the Irrationality of Ideology. All social change involves some element of ambiguity, but not always to the same degree. Once the initial information is in, a disaster presents a relatively unambiguous situation: the causes are clear, and the consequences obvious. In contrast, most social change is more ambiguous. The Great Depression of the 1930's threw many people out of work, but no man knew its cause or corrction. When ambiguity is combined with stress, as in economic depression, the situation is indeed difficult: action is urgently needed, yet the perspectives which guide effective action are hard to come by. Many social changes are like projective tests: the individual has to make sense of an unclear situation. We know what happens when people are asked to describe an ambiguous inkblot: in part their answers are conditioned by the form of the blot—objectively, it may indeed look rather like a bird or bat—but also their answers are conditioned by their needs, expectations, interests, defenses, and fears. Much of the same process takes place in interpreting the ambiguities of the social situation. Faced with unclear social change, a multitude of beliefs and perceptions may develop, of greater or lesser coherence and rationality. Sometimes the emergent perspectives may be very simple indeed; they only verbalize and direct a dominant mood. The notions of "black power," "police brutality," and "soul-brother," which played so central a role in the Negro riots of 1967, were such simple beliefs. But sometimes perspectives are exceedingly complicated; they may provide an articulated view of history, an ego-gratifying definition of one's own groups as the chosen people, a redefinition of personal identity, a complex prescription for action, and a prophetic formula for the millennium. This kind of coherent, articulated, and complex perspective is generally referred to as "ideology"; the ideologies of communism, fascism, and the Black Muslims are examples. But simple or complex the need is the same: to define the nature of stressful change and to direct action toward resolving the strain.

Given social ambiguity, and given the shared needs and fears which influence interpretation, the perspectives or ideologies which emerge often appear to others as tangential or irrelevant. The status insecurities of a poorly educated businessman may lead to membership in a right-wing anti-Communist crusade, and to beliefs far removed from any objectively effective action (Chesler, Schmuck and Whiteside, 1965). The exploited sharecropper may join a pentecostal movement whose ideology makes no reference to the sources of his exploitation (Boisen, 1939). The beliefs of a Negro Black Muslim may be illusory, and remote from historical truth (Lincoln, 1961).

Such discrepancies between the objective social situation and the new perspectives are often striking, and sometimes bizarre. Ever since Le Bon (1896) wrote so feelingly about the irrationality of crowds, psychologists and sociologists have been impressed by this discrepancy. Studies of rumors have focused mainly upon the distortions and oddities of the rumor process. Psychologists have tended to view ideologies as if they were projective test responses, while political scientists have explained conservative and utopian ideologies as a justification for class interest. Undeniably there are strong grounds for this emphasis upon the disguised and the seemingly irrational.

Yet not always are the emergent perspectives entirely illusory. For example, rumors may serve as a relatively valid source of information (Schachter and Burdick, 1955; Diggory, 1956; Caplow, 1947), and lead to collective decisions (Shibutani, 1966; Turner and Killian, 1957). Marxist insights about historical process have been widely accepted by non-Communist scholars. Ideological prescriptions for action may be realistic: the works of Mao Tse-tung on guerrilla warfare and the Leninist writings on organizational infiltration are the classic "how-to" texts for revolution. Even science may be regarded as an alternative to earlier myth-based ideologies: science too defines the nature of reality and suggests means to action.

In general, we would suspect that perspectives will be the more irrational as the source of stress is more ambiguous. Beliefs are irrational simply because relevant information is not available, or because the receiver cannot utilize it. On the other hand, a relatively clear threat or crisis is less likely to give rise to irrational belief.

For most of Topeka, the tornado posed little ambiguity. Yet this was not the total reaction. When a group of East Topekans felt that they had been slighted by helping activities and by the mass media, their protest was predicated not alone upon the objective situation. Theirs was a low-income area with poor housing and high unemployment. It was easy for them to feel that they would get short shrift, and to respond accordingly, quite apart from the objective reality.

The Role of Perspectives in the Mobilization of Collective Action. So far we have spoken of perspectives as a result of a social process. People look to others for factual information, they seek new ideas from discussion. The perspectives are elaborated and revised through a process of social communication. Yet this collective process alone is not enough to lead to collective action. We shall next consider the route by which perspectives led to the mobilization of collective action in Topeka.

The prime prerequisite for organization is the existence of shared tasks, which opens the way for group development. But this is not the only prerequisite. For instance, although most victims shared the task of warding off fear and anxiety, this seldom formed the basis for organized social activity. Thus the existence of shared tasks was a necessary but not a sufficient condition for mobilizing action.

A second prerequisite is that these shared tasks can be communicated. If people with similar tasks are out of contact with each other, group formation is unlikely. Or if for some reason people are hesitant to communicate information about shared tasks, groups are not likely to develop. Spontaneous group formation necessarily implies not only that tasks are shared, but that people perceive them to be shared.

A third prerequisite is that group activity is available as a means of task accomplishment. Many people outside the tornado area wanted to do something, but "did not know how." They were forced to sit by until they heard that a Volunteer Center was in operation, or that a collection point for clothes was available. In other cases would-be helpers were able to make use of previously existing groups and develop them to meet new needs—as Mrs. Brown did with her church. Only when the means of group activity were available could groups develop.

But the option of group activity is not likely to be taken up unless a fourth prerequisite is also met—group efforts must be perceived as uniquely effective in meeting high priority tasks. Such perception depends upon both objective and subjective factors. Some welfare workers who came to volunteer for group activity became disillusioned; they were more concerned about the fate of the people on their caseload, and less concerned about the helping activities engaged in by the volunteer group. The group activity was irrelevant to their own system of priorities, and they withdrew into individual effort whenever possible. Others, as in the work crew described in Chapter 4, found that group activity had a clear advantage, and they stayed.

These additive, ordered processes necessary to group formation may be diagramed as follows:

shared common tasks of high priority	+	communication and perception of the shared nature of the task	+	joint task-oriented activity available as a means of task accomplishment
+	joint action perceived as more effective	→	social group formation	

When these four processes occur, groups will arise spontaneously to deal with the tasks of disaster recovery.[4]

We may also use this diagram to describe various ways in which people *did not* engage in collective action. We have noted that some individuals lacked any feeling of empathic involvement with the victims—this is another way of saying that they simply did not share the common task. Others were unable to find satisfactory means of task accomplishment, even when they perceived joint action to be an effective technique. Still others felt, from their perspectives and in terms of the needs confronting them, that individual action would be a more appropriate vehicle for providing help—this was commonly the case with people who had families in the disaster area and were therefore mainly concerned with providing immediate relief to kin. It was only a select subgroup for whom these four contingencies were met, and who were available to take part in the formation of volunteer social groups.

[4] At this level of analysis, the study of collective behavior merges with organizational theory. The classic exposition is given by Barnard (1938, p. 82): "An organization comes into being when (1) there are persons able to communicate with others (2) who are willing to contribute action (3) to accomplish a common purpose." Many of our specific observations of post-tornado organization may be seen as special cases of the general process hypothesized by Barnard.

THE MOBILIZATION OF COLLECTIVE BEHAVIOR
AND THE EMERGENCE OF LEADERSHIP

For a group to mobilize effectively, some form of preliminary structure is helpful. Leadership is necessary to supply this structure. In Topeka, two kinds of leaders emerged to provide structure and mobilize action: the legitimate leaders whose organizational responsibilities put them in the forefront of mobilization activities, and other leaders who emerged without formal sanction. The mayor provides an example of the socially sanctioned leadership, Bob Harder of leadership arising *de novo*. The leader needs to be aware of strategic options; he needs to know how to find workers, tools, and services. Leadership also demands coordination of service and efforts, especially when the old channels and procedures for coordination are no longer sufficient. An awareness of strategic options, plus the need for coordination, led immediately to the formation of the ephermeral government, as described in Chapter 6. At a lower level of leadership, we have seen how school principals and ordinary citizens took on leadership functions when the tasks demanded them, even though they had no official sanctions for doing so. It was this kind of leadership at different levels of task complexity which provided the organizational matrix for the growth of group behavior.

In a crisis situation the way seems unusually open for the development of new leadership patterns and roles. Harder has described how his orders were followed unquestioningly even though he had no particular expertise in his field of operation. Similarly, in the Red Cross center, a "take charge man" appeared from nowhere to organize the activities. High school girls managed kitchens; a school principal acted as coordinator for work crews. There was a suspension of challenge—in Barnard's (1938) terms, the zone of indifference was unusually wide. Anyone who provided a plan was followed with minimal questioning.

A similar "suspension of challenge" is commonly noted in other forms of collective behavior. Cantril (1941), for instance, speaks of heightened suggestibility when people en masse are confronted by critical situations. The reason is obvious: when tasks are pressing and their solution unclear, anyone who can offer a halfway reasonable strategy is welcome. In order to offer an acceptable strategy, the leader must in part share the perspectives of his potential followers, otherwise his direction appears irrelevant. Thus a certain "identification" (Cantril, 1941), a certain perception of the leader as embodying the frustrations and hopes of the mass (Green, 1964) is necessary. Especially are these issues pronounced with leaders who are seen as more than human; in Hertzler's (1957, p. 370) terms, the emergence of a self-confident decision maker who acts to remove doubt and ambiguity allows "distraught and humiliated individuals [to] merge themselves with something which is assertive, powerful, and reputedly invincible." No such charismatic leader emerged from the tornado, in part because the crisis was soon over. The tornado did, however, provide a small-scale view of the social dynamics which, if writ large, could produce such a leader.

FEEDBACK AND SECONDARY STRAIN

In this new organizational matrix, groups formed and set about their tasks. As people became involved in the group process, as they attempted to fulfill new social tasks and interact with victims, their roles developed, grew more complex, and often changed in unexpected ways. We may view these changes as feedback phenomena: the result of action and reaction in human encounter. The influence of feedback emerges most clearly from our observation of the volunteer work groups.

Any group of individuals engaged in a collective task takes on the task of working amicably with one another. Frictions may develop within the group, conflicts of choice will emerge, and these will threaten the integrity of the group. Thus the continuation of the group requires that attention be given to the tasks of group maintenance. It is common for groups to work out ways of channeling or blocking interpersonal tensions; common, in fact, for groups to develop specific subroles, so that one member plays the part of conciliator, another the part of the humorist. The tasks of group maintenance, being shared, being fed back to individuals, influence the formation of roles.

Secondly, new feedbacks arise because a group is a categorized object. Those outside the group perceive the group to be an entity in itself, and react to it in ways different from their reactions to individuals. The group as a *group* has to work out its course of action in the social world. Such feedbacks and responses help to define and sanction group membership, while at the same time posing new tasks. Thus the work crew came to develop a sense of group identity—sometimes even a sense of "us against them." It became a group in part because of internal cooperation, but also in part because of the ever-present need to define what it was and what it could do for a sequence of potential "clients."

Finally, the group may provide a means for avoiding or handling unanticipated strains. For instance, the volunteers typically found themselves troubled by the existence of "unworthy victims": victims who failed to cooperate, who sat idly by while the volunteers did all the work, who attempted to "take advantage" of the helpers. If the group was to work effectively, it had to deal with the task of maintaining morale in the face of such negative experiences. Within the work group it was possible to develop a set of attitudes and behaviors which gave comfort in such situations. The Mennonite work crews often volunteered to help homeowners only, avoiding renters, on the (generally valid) assumption that owners would be more involved and grateful. The work crew described in Chapter 4 came to focus more upon the job as a test of workmanlike skill, and to de-emphasize the personal transactions between helper and victim. Such ways of dealing with the new task were made easier when buttressed by group consensus and support.

Thus, the role of helper, as it emerged in the group setting, involved an increasing differentiation among tasks and means; an increasing specialization; and an increasing intermingling of the external tasks of tornado recovery, the internal tasks of group maintenance, the tasks posed by new contingencies.

It is likely that this small work crew has similarities with other kinds of collective behavior; there too new roles emerge within a group process. Unfortunately, we know of no comparable analysis of the development of role in other forms of collective behavior. An analogue—but a rather vague one—is provided by the changes sometimes seen in small sects as they develop over time, take on new members, and become more differentiated and "church-like." Such sects show an increased differentiation of roles, and increased specialization.

CURTAIN CALL

We have in this volume attempted to look in an interdisciplinary, organismic way at the phenomenon of a single disaster. We have examined the individual actors in the disaster drama, the reactions of formal organizations, and the growth of ephemeral and innovative institutions. This analysis has led finally to a larger focus: to a consideration of other forms of discontinuous social change. Thus we have moved from a microscopic focus on individual response to a macroscopic focus on historical behavior under conditions of stress. We have attempted to show that similar phenomena, and possibly similar processes, characterize other forms of collective behavior.

It is tempting at this point to write *finis* to the discussion, to close with a sense of completion. Yet such a denouement leaves us still dissatisfied. We have contributed perhaps to an understanding of collective behavior, but the study of collective behavior itself is in a remarkably unsatisfactory state; it remains an inchoate and undigestible topic within the social sciences. It is not really a discipline in its own right, with its own phenomena and paradigms; rather it is a mixed bag of topics yearning for a place in sociology and social psychology. In spite of a few attempts to introduce conceptual order into the field (most recently by the sociologist, Smelser, 1962, and the psychologist, Toch, 1965), the major problems, issues, and scientific concepts remain only half developed, and only tangentially linked to the parent disciplines.

In part this reflects a more general problem. Auguste Comte long ago pointed to the difference between the study of social statics and the study of social dynamics: the former concerned with the maintenance of social order and regularity, the latter with the processes which lead to change, growth, and discontinuity. Except where contemporary American sociology has been influenced by Marxism and its derivatives, it has mainly been concerned with statics. A rich and interdigitated descriptive terminology has been developed, along with the beginnings of larger theory, in describing the conditions of social order and regularity. No such extended development has taken place for the study of dynamic change. Without such theoretical undergirding, the study of collective behavior as a form of social change has withered.[5]

We are in no position to remedy this lack. Yet in striving for an organismic view of collective behavior, we have been led to consider the ways in which certain key notions in sociology, notions which are usually used in describing homeostatic phenomena, may be extended so as to be useful as well in describing the dynamics of change. It seems worth while to develop these thoughts in more detail, not in order to develop a full-fledged "theory of collective behavior," but as a small contribution to the eventual building of such a theory. In our earlier discussion

[5] In pointing to this basic "conservative" bias in sociology we do not wish to imply that no sociologists have been or are concerned with the theory of social change. Currently there is a re-emergent interest in the analysis of social change, and in the development of a dynamic sociology which views man not as a social pawn in a game wherein the rules of play are governed by normative consensus, but rather as a striving, complexly motivated creature who negotiates, bargains, reciprocates, and on occasion rebels. The controversy between the two points of view is well summarized by Buckley (1967, pp. 127–61 *passim*); and most recently Etzioni (1968) has attempted a massive reformulation of social and political theory in dynamic, action terms. Others too have attempted to introduce notions of exchange and motivation into social theory: cf. particularly Thibaut and Kelley (1959), Homans (1961), Blau (1964), and Nord (1969).

the notion of "role" has been central; in the following paragraphs we shall attempt to show how the study of roles might be extended to encompass certain phenomena of collective behavior.

Roles in the "Living Theater." In ordinary sociological usage, the term "role" refers to the behavior expected of a person who occupies a particular social status. The domain of role study is:

> . . . nothing more nor less than complex, real-life behavior as it is displayed in genuine on-going social situations. Role analysts examine such problems as the processes and phases of socialization, interdependences among individuals, the characteristics and organization of social positions, processes of conformity and sanctioning, specialization of performance and the division of labor, and many others [Biddle and Thomas, 1966, p. 17].

The field of role study is greatly influenced by its underlying metaphor, a metaphor which suggests that the world is a stage and that the individuals thereon are acting out a more or less predetermined script. This dramaturgic metaphor usefully brings together such sociological concepts as norms, social position, and social behavior. By analogy, the social world provides the script which the individual actor follows as he presents a unique interpretation before his particular audience. Although the language of role theory has been much augmented in recent years by proliferating terminology—including such technical terms as "actor," "alter," "ego," "alter casting," "coaching," "backstage"—the basic metaphor remains unchanged.

Yet the metaphor has its limitations. With it, "Man is increasingly seen as a role playing creature, responding eagerly or anxiously to the expectations of other role players in the multiple group settings in which he finds himself" (Wrong, 1961, p. 190). His acts are created by social norms and social expectations; his highest goals are the goals of social conformity; his anguish and tensions arise only when the performance demands exceed his capacity, or are incompatible one with another. There is little room in this passive conception for the human being of our everyday experience—that active, questing, goal-oriented, tragicomic character who chooses and demands, accepts and rejects, who is himself his own most easily fooled audience and his own most unforgiving critic.

The phenomena of disaster confront us starkly with this basic limitation in the dramaturgic analogy. When disaster strikes it disrupts the audience, the transactions, the norms, and the sets of expectations which make up the social order. Yet new roles arise by the processes spelled out in the preceding pages; the forms of these roles are actively created by the tasks which individuals set, or fail to set, for themselves.

This situation has no analogy with the classic theater. It is more akin to the so-called "Living Theater" wherein the actors, responding to the audience, will create from their own empathy and observation the form and drama of their performance. In these newer forms of theater, the actor's choice is large: he accepts or rejects a task—suggested perhaps by the audience, or by the other players, or by himself—and in his scriptless performance he creates a role by drawing upon his own skills, his own potentials, and the external resources of his stage and cast. Here is the dramatic art which, we would suggest, provides the quintessential metaphor for discontinuous collective change.

We have thus thought it useful, in our discussion of individual, group, and organizational roles, to augment the usual passive terminology of role description by introducing more active concepts. We have been led to emphasize aspects of motivation, of choice, of bargaining and reciprocity.[6] From the perspective of social change, the important thing about social positions and roles is not that they are expectable, but that they are purposive. They are focused around tasks—here broadly defined as the hoped-

---

[6] This emphasis represents an attempt to link role theory to such emergent sociological concepts as "exchange," "bargaining," "negotiation," and "games." The need for such linkage is well expressed by Turner: "Role theory, originally depicting a tentative and creative interaction process, has come increasingly to be employed as a refinement of conformity theory. In consequence, the theory has become relatively sterile except with respect to the consequences of role conflict and other forms of deviation from the conventional model of role behavior . . . Conformity to perceived expectations is but one special way in which an actor's role-playing may be related to the role of relevant others" (1962, p. 37–38).

for accomplishments, the goal orientations, of individual or group action. They develop in response to available options, constraints, and payoffs. It is the agreed-upon set of tasks which is central to the role: all else simply defines the arena and the audience participation. For example, in viewing the victims, we have been led to look at the many tasks imposed upon them by disaster: the shared yet private tasks of mastering discordant feelings and their fate in the disaster landscape, as well as the shared and public tasks of reciprocation with would-be helpers, helping agencies, and the sightseers of disaster. Similarly, in order to understand the dynamics of group and organizational change, we have been led to look at the tasks imposed by the tornado on nonvictims, at the ways in which such tasks were avoided or carried forward, and at the options or assets provided by the pre-existing social structure. In other forms of collective behavior too the emergent roles build and grow around the tasks imposed by social change. In short, social change produces new social and psychological tasks, and the new set of tasks provides the seed-crystal for newly emergent roles, groups, and organizations.

The development of such new roles is not frozen by the initial set of tasks, any more than the form of a developing crystal is frozen by the form of its seed. We have noted how, in the emergent social phenomena, increased specialization and external feedback led to new tasks and new resolutions. So too with most collective behavior: the development of new social forms gives rise to new stress, to new collective tasks and to new role bargains, adaptations, and differentiations. A role may thus be conceived as a cybernetic system, a system in which social change influences not only the behavioral input and output, but also the governing regulator—the set of tasks itself.

Socialization and Desocialization. In contemporary social theory the notion of role is integrally linked with a second notion, that of socialization. If a role is conceived as a set of expected status behaviors, socialization may be conceived as the process by which a person learns such expectations, statuses, and behaviors. *"The function of socialization is to transform the raw material of society into good working members;* the content can be considered analytically to include an understanding of the society's status structure and of the role prescriptions and behavior associated with the different positions in this structure" (Brim and Wheeler, 1966, p. 5; italics added). Through the process of socialization, man as a passive creature is molded into the shape demanded by society. Much socialization theory, like much role theory, emphasizes social order, homeostasis, and consensus. The student of socialization "asks how the work of society gets done and how the necessary manpower is trained, motivated, kept alive and functioning throughout the life cycle so that specific roles are performed" (ibid., p. 5). He does not ask how roles break down, how role behavior changes, and what happens when "the work of society" is disrupted.

We suggest that the notion of a "socialization process" might usefully be balanced by another notion: the notion of a "desocialization process." Socialization refers to those events which push the individual to *take on* prescribed role tasks, values, perspectives, and behaviors. Desocialization, by contrast, would refer to those processes which push the individual to *give up or modify* his role tasks, values, perspectives, and behaviors. Socialization implies the learning of new role patterns, desocialization the giving up of old ones. "Socialization" speaks to the stability and continuity of roles within a predictable social world; "desocialization" speaks to the instability and discontinuity of role behavior in the face of social or personal change. Just as the analysis of social stability and disorder leads us to emphasize the process of socialization, so does the analysis of instability and disorder lead us to emphasize the process of desocialization. Since society is always changing, the study of socialization has its necessary counterpart in the study of desocialization; the two are inextricably mixed.

One way of looking at the stress of disaster is to view it as an abrupt and acute desocialization experience. From this perspective, the first three chapters of this book are concerned with the process of ephemeral desocialization and its effects on individuals. Similarly, the social stresses which lead to other kinds of collective behavior can be viewed as less abrupt but more long-lasting forms of desocialization.

The pressures of desocialization force the abandonment of particular and much practiced roles. They do so by removing the usual opportunities for role reward, or by decreasing the possibility of negative sanctions, or by imposing sets of tasks which cannot be fulfilled by the usual role behaviors. All of these desocialization processes were encountered after the tornado, as they are in most episodes of collective behavior.

Obviously there are degrees of desocialization. The pressures for role abandonment or change may be mild, as when new civil rights legislation outlaws overt discrimination in hiring. Or the pressures may be major, as when economic depression leads to abrupt loss of income and function. This may affect only one role, or many roles. In the latter case, it is likely that the impact will be pervasive, that the individual will feel not only a sense of deprivation but also a disruption of identity. We saw minor examples of this occasionally after the tornado, and similar observations are made of people attracted to political or religious movements. We may understand this by regarding the identity as a kind of superordinate organizing role, which overlaps and gives coherence to the specific behaviors of many more specific roles. Indeed, it is precisely when the pressures of desocialization are most pervasive that individuals are led to seek new identities within the embrace of a totalistic social movement.

Under certain conditions, as discussed earlier in this chapter, the emergent social tasks, options, and contingencies lead individuals to group action, and existing institutions to realign their commitments. Sometimes, when there is agreement on perspectives and tasks, the result is what we saw in the post-disaster Utopia: a collective mood of brotherhood and high morale. More commonly, social change will produce rather different forms of desocialization in differing groups, depending on their pre-existing placement in the social structure. As a result, different groups may give primacy to different and conflicting tasks, with the resulting clash at times leading to further desocialization. A small-scale example of this was seen in the encounter between the bureaucratic adaptation of the Red Cross and the activist adaptation of the Volunteer Center, an encounter which led the volunteer workers to elaborate their own roles in contradistinction to the "starched ladies" from the Red Cross. A similar process of dialectic is basic to most collective behavior. Thus the policeman and the student activist are both influenced by social change; each is subject to desocialization pressures, each in response redefines his tasks and options—yet with a vast divergence. Encounters between student activists and police may produce further pressures in both toward role change. As in every social movement, the clash of discordant roles breeds a polarity. Such considerations, however, move us to the more complex issues of social change, of class conflict and consensus, of bargaining and coalition, of historical flow and change; issues which transcend the scope of role theory, the study of disaster—and this book.

REFERENCES

ABEL, T. *The Nazi movement*. New York: Atherton Press, 1965.

BAKER, G. W., and CHAPMAN, D. W. (eds.). *Man and society in disaster*. New York: Basic Books, 1962.

BAKST, H. J., BERG, R., FOSTER, F. D., and RAKER, J. Report on the Worcester, Massachusetts tornado. Washington, D.C.: National Research Council–National Academy of Sciences, 1953. Mimeographed.

BARNARD, C. I. *The functions of the executive*. Cambridge, Mass.: Harvard University Press, 1938.

BARTON, A. H. The emergency social system. In Baker and Chapman (eds.), *Man and society in disaster*. Pp. 222–67.

BECKER, H. S., GEER, BLANCHE, HUGHES, E. C., and STRAUSS, A. L. *Boys in white: Student culture in medical school*. Chicago: University of Chicago Press, 1961.

BIDDLE, B. J., and THOMAS, E. J. *Role theory*. New York: Wiley, 1966.

BLAU, P. M. *Exchange and power in social life*. New York: Wiley, 1964.

BLUM, R. H., and KLASS, B. A study of public response to disaster warnings. Stanford Research Institute, June 1956. Unpublished. Cited in Fritz and Williams, The human being in disasters.

BLUMER, H. Collective behavior. In A. M. Lee (ed.), *Principles of sociology.* New York: Barnes and Noble, 1951, pp. 167–222.

BOISEN, A. T. Economic distress and religious experience: A study of the Holy Rollers. *Psychiatry,* 1939, 2:185–94.

BRIM, O. G., JR., and WHEELER, S. *Socialization after childhood: Two essays.* New York: Wiley, 1966.

BRINTON, C. *The anatomy of revolution.* New York: Vintage, 1952.

BUCKLEY, W. *Sociology and modern systems theory.* Englewood Cliffs, N.J.: Prentice-Hall, 1967.

CANTRIL, H. *The psychology of social movements.* New York: Wiley, 1941.

CAPLOW, T. Rumors in war. *Social Forces,* 1947, 25:298–302.

CHAPMAN, D. W. A brief introduction to contemporary disaster research. In Baker and Chapman (eds.), *Man and society in disaster.* Pp. 3–22.

CHESLER, M., Schmuck, R., and WHITESIDE, J. Social backgrounds and personality predispositions of super-patriots. Paper read at Society for the Psychological Studies of Social Issues, Chicago, 1965. Available from Institute of Social Research, University of Michigan. 10 pp., dittoed.

COHN, N. *The pursuit of the millennium.* Fairlawn, N.J.: Essential Books, 1957.

DAVIS, A. Acculturation in schools. In M. L. Barron (ed.), *American Minorities.* New York: Knopf, 1957, pp. 446–49.

DEMERATH, N. J. Some general propositions: An interpretive summary. In N. J. Demerath and A. F. C. Wallace (eds.), Human adaptation to disaster. *Human Organization* (special issue), 1957, 16, No. 2:28–29.

DEUTSCH, M. An experimental study of the effects of cooperation upon group process. *Human Relations,* 1949, 2:199–231.

DEUTSCHER, I., and NEW, K. Report on the Ruskin Heights, Missouri, tornado. Washington, D.C.: National Research Council-National Academy of Sciences, 1957. Mimeographed.

DIGGORY, J. C. Some consequences of proximity to a disease threat. *Sociometry,* 1956, 19:47–53.

DRAYER, C. S., CAMERON, D. C., WOODWARD, W. D., and GLASS, A. J. *Psychological first aid in community disasters.* Washington, D.C.: American Psychiatric Association, Committee on Civil Defense, 1954.

DURKHEIM, E. *The division of labor in society,* trans. George Simpson. Glencoe, Ill.: Free Press, 1947.

DYNES, R. R., and QUARANTELLI, E. L. Group behavior under stress: A required convergence of organizational and collective behavior perspectives. *Sociology and Social Research,* 1968, 52:416–29.

ENGEL, G. L. *Psychological development in health and disease.* Philadelphia: Saunders, 1962.

ERIKSON, E. H. The problem of ego identity. *Journal of the American Psychoanalytic Association,* 1956, 4:56–121.

ETZIONI, A. *The active society.* New York: Free Press, 1968.

FORM, W. H., and Nosow, S. *Community in disaster.* New York: Harper and Brothers, 1958.

FRITZ, C. E. Disaster. In R. K. Merton and R. A. Nisbet (eds.), *Contemporary social problems.* New York: Harcourt, Brace, 1961, pp. 651–94.

———, and Marks, E. S. The NORC studies of human behavior in disaster. In D. W. Chapman (ed.), Human behavior in disaster: A new field of social research. *Journal of Social Issues,* 1954, 10, No. 3:26–41.

———, and Williams, H. B. The human being in disasters: A research perspective. *Annals of the American Academy of Political and Social Science,* 1957, 309:42–51.

GLASS, A. J. Psychological aspects of disaster. *Journal of the American Medical Association,* 1959, 171:222–25.

GREEN, A. W. *Sociology; an analysis of life in modern society.* 4th ed. New York: McGraw-Hill, 1964.

GUSFIELD, J. R. Organizational change: A study of the Womens' Christian Temperance Union. Ph.D. dissertation, University of Chicago, 1954.

HEBB, D. O. The motivating effects of exteroceptive stimulation. *American Psychologist,* 1958, 13:109–13.

HERMANN, MARGARET G. *Stress, self-esteem, and defensiveness in an inter-nation simulation.* Ph.D. dissertation, Northwestern University. Ann Arbor, Mich.: University Microfilms, 1965, No. 65–12099.

HERTZLER, J. O. Crises and dictatorships. In R. H. Turner and L. M. Killian, *Collective behavior.* Englewood Cliffs, N.J.: Prentice-Hall, 1957, pp. 364–74.

HOMANS, G. C. *Social behavior: Its elementary forms.* New York: Harcourt, Brace, and World, 1961.

JANIS, I. L. *Psychological stress.* New York: Wiley, 1958.

JANOWITZ, M., and LITTLE, R. *Sociology and the military establishment.* Rev. ed. New York: Russell Sage Foundation, 1965.

KILLIAN, L. M. Some accomplishments and some needs in disaster studies. In D. W. Chapman (ed.). Human behavior in disaster: A new field of social research. *Journal of Social Issues,* 1954, 10, No. 3:66–72.

KRUGMAN, H. J. The appeal of communism to American middle-class intellectuals and trade unionists. *Public Opinion Quarterly,* 1952, 16:331–55.

KUBZANSKY, P. E., and LANDERMAN, P. H. Sensory deprivation: An overview. In P. Solomon *et al.* (eds.), *Sensory deprivation.* Cambridge, Mass.: Harvard University Press, 1961, pp. 221–38.

LE BON, G. *The crowd.* New York: Macmillan, 1896.

LEWIN, K. Problems of group dynamics and the integration of the social sciences: I. Social Equilibria. *Journal of Human Relations,* 1947, 1:5–41.

LINCOLN, C. E. *The Black Muslims in America.* Boston: Beacon Press, 1961.

MEAD, MARGARET. *New lives for old.* New York: Morrow, 1956.

MENNINGER, K. A. Psychological aspects of the organism under stress. Part II: Regulatory devices of the ego under major stress. *Journal of the American Psychoanalytic Association,* 1954, 2:280–310.

MENNINGER, W. C. Psychological reactions in an emergency (flood). *American Journal of Psychiatry,* 1952, 109, No. 2:128–30.

MERTON, R. K. *Social theory and social structure.* Glencoe, Ill.: Free Press, 1957.

MOORE, H. E. *Tornadoes over Texas.* Austin: University of Texas Press, 1958.

NORD, W. R. Social exchange theory: An integrative approach to social conformity. *Psychological Bulletin,* 1969, 71:174–209.

POWELL, J. W., Finesinger, J. E., and Greenhill, M. H. An introduction to the natural history of disaster. Vol. II: Final contract report, Disaster Research Project. College Park: University of Maryland, Psychiatric Institute, 1954. Unpublished.

RAPAPORT, D. Theory of autonomy: A generalization. *Bulletin of the Menninger Clinic,* 1958, 22:13–35.

SCHACHTER, S., and BURDICK, H. A field experiment in rumor transmission and distortion. *Journal of Abnormal and Social Psychology,* 1955, 50:363–71.

SHASKOLSKY, L. Volunteerism in disaster situations. Paper No. 10, Disaster Research Center, Ohio State University, undated. Mimeographed.

SHERIF, M. HARVEY, O. J., WHITE, B. J., HOOD, W. R., and SHERIF, CAROLYN. Experimental study of positive and negative ingroup attitudes between experimentally produced groups: Robbers cave study. Intergroup Relations Project, University of Oklahoma, 1954. Mimeographed.

SHIBUTANI, T. *Improvised news.* Indianapolis: Bobbs-Merrill, 1966.

SMELSER, N. J. *Theory of collective behavior.* London: Routledge and Kegan Paul, 1962.

THIBAUT, J. W., and KELLEY, H. H. *The social psychology of groups.* New York: Wiley, 1959.

THOMAS, E. J. Effects of facilitative role interdependence on group functioning. *Human Relations,* 1957, 10:347–66.

THOMPSON, J. D., and HAWKES, R. W. Disaster community organization and administrative process. In Baker and Chapman (eds.), *Man and society in disaster.* Pp. 268–300.

TOCH, H. *The social psychology of social movements.* Indianapolis: Bobbs-Merrill, 1965.

TOPEKA *Daily Capital,* June 16, 1966.

TURNER, R. H. Role-taking: Process versus conformity. In A. M. Rose (ed.), *Human behavior and social processes: An interactionist approach.* Boston, Mass.: Houghton Mifflin, 1962, pp. 20–40.

――――. Types of solidarity in the reconstituting of groups. Expanded version of paper presented at the annual meeting of the American Sociological Association, Miami Beach, Fla., August 1966. Mimeographed.

――――, and Killian, L. M. *Collective behavior.* Englewood Cliffs, N.J.: Prentice-Hall, 1957.

TYHURST, J. S. Individual reactions to community disaster. *American Journal of Psychiatry,* 1951, 107:764–69.

WALLACE, A. F. C. Mazeway disintegration: The individual's perception of sociocultural disorganization. In J. Demerath and A. F. C. Wallace (eds.), Human adaptation to disaster. *Human Organization* (special issue), 1957, 16, No. 2:23–27.

――――. *Tornado in Worcester.* Disaster Study No. 3, Publication 392. Washington, D.C.: National Research Council–National Academy of Sciences, 1956.

WHITE, R. K. (ed.). *The study of lives: Essays on personality in honor of Henry A. Murray.* New York: Basic Books, 1963.

WITHEY, S. B. Reaction to uncertain threat. In Baker and Chapman (eds.), *Man and society in disaster.* Pp. 93–123.

WOLFENSTEIN, MARTHA. *Disaster: A psychological essay.* Glencoe, Ill.: Free Press, 1957.

WRONG, D. H. The oversocialized conception of man in modern society. *American Sociological Review,* 1961, 26:183–93.

ZURCHER, L. A. Social-psychological functions of ephemeral roles: A disaster work crew. *Human Organization,* 1968, 27:281–97.

SUBJECT INDEX

AUTHOR INDEX